A Journey of Voices
Chasing the Frontier

Diane McAdams Gladow

Cover Image: William H. Jordan's land in Bienville Parish, Louisiana.

"A Journey of Voices: Chasing the Frontier," by Diane McAdams Gladow. ISBN 978-1-60264-531-8.

Published 2010 by Virtualbookworm.com Publishing Inc., P.O. Box 9949, College Station, TX 77842, US. ©2010, Diane McAdams Gladow. All rights reserved. No part of this publication may be reproduced, stored in a retrieval system, or transmitted in any form or by any means, electronic, mechanical, recording or otherwise, without the prior written permission of Diane McAdams Gladow.

Manufactured in the United States of America.

Dedication

In order for a book like this to exist, people have to save things. In every generation, there must be a "keeper," a person who keeps things and passes them on. My family is truly fortunate to have had a keeper in each generation since the early 1800s on both my mother and father's side. With every generation of my mother's family, the keeper's surname changed, but the treasures were still saved and handed down. Although everyone cannot be a keeper or we would never be able to get through the doors of our houses, I salute the ones who are and were. Thanks to them, we who live in the present are able to put flesh on the bones of our ancestors and begin to understand who they were, and, in the process, who we are as well. This book is dedicated to my family's "keepers" – Martha Jordan, Margaret Jane Jordan Ferguson, Nora Ferguson Crume, and Gladys Crume McAdams.

Chapter 1

"Whatcha doin', Mama?" I asked.

"Lookin' through this old trunk," my mother replied. Mom knelt on her hands and knees beside a large hump-back trunk, the wood and metal fittings dark and battered with age. She had the lid open and was removing papers, books, and a number of strange objects. Being a curious nine-year-old, I wanted to know about the trunk and its contents.

"What's in there?"

"The past," my mother murmured.

"What's the past?" I continued to press for answers as my nose wrinkled up from a strange smell. I quickly pinched it closed with my fingers.

"It's the things that long-ago people treasured enough to save and pack away in a safe place."

"Why did they like this old stuff?"

"Because they loved the people who owned these things, and it was all they had left after the people died," Mother tried to explain, knowing it was impossible for a nine-year-old to understand.

"Did they save these things for us to have?" I asked.

"I don't think they thought about that at the time. They just wanted to hold onto their loved ones," my mother mused as she sorted items into neat piles.

Beginning to lose interest, my final comment on my mother's project, as I held my nose, was, "The past sure stinks!" Mom laughed and said, "It sure does. Really old things always smell bad - musty and moldy." Mom dove back into her work, and I slipped away to more important occupations.

Thus began my family's long journey into the past, a journey to discover the people who had come before us, their lives, their treasured keepsakes, and even their voices. First my mother succumbed to the journey's lure, my father and brother followed, and finally it captured me as well. Two very old hump-back trunks began our adventure, one representing my father's family line and one my mother's. The trunks, packed with the treasures of several generations, lovingly saved and handed down, yielded the clues that eventually unlocked the past.

The memorabilia collected in the old trunks belonged to families who bore common characteristics. They immigrated to America from the British Isles - Scotland, Ireland, England, and Wales. Upon reaching the new world, they grouped themselves together with other families from the home countries, married each other's children, and traveled across America together - always seeking a better place. Common character traits were stubbornness and pride, and these often helped them persevere in troubled times. Laughter helped to heal their sadness and made bearable their sometimes poverty-stricken condition. They loved the land, and they loved music. Although they were highly religious, they rarely forgave an insult - in typical Scotch-Irish fashion. They protected their families no matter what the cost, and they were fierce fighters in many cases. They believed in God, and they believed in themselves; they had to hold these beliefs in order to survive. Included in the great mass of common people who built a new nation and saw it through some rough times, they lived each day as it came, made what they could out of it, and didn't dwell in the past. However, some of them tried to save small bits of that past, the bits that were connected to family.

Once the trunks revealed their treasures, the objects inside became as familiar to me growing up as my dolls or toys. I never thought it unusual to see a Civil War vintage letter lying on the dining room table ready to be transcribed. An old "last" used for constructing shoes during the Civil War served as a doorstop. Genealogical records and old pictures in piles covered the dining room desk. However, of all the objects preserved in the old trunks, the pliers used to pull teeth fascinated me the most. Old family stories related that the pliers had been used by ancestor land owners to "cure" their workers' tooth maladies. Antiquated eyeglasses and pipes, straight razors, watch chains, Bibles, school books and slates, and even a paint set became familiar objects to charge the imagination.

"Come look at these things and let me tell you who they belonged to." My mother was trying again to stir up in me some interest for the old keepsakes.

"OK," I mumbled unenthusiastically. I didn't want to disappoint her, but a high school student has important things to do, and at this time of my life, I had only marginal interest in the old trunks' contents. Dead certain that I would never remember what things belonged to which ancestor, I nonetheless listened to the old stories once again.

After an hour or so of listening, I finally said, "Mom, you better write down the history which goes with each one of these things and tag them because I'm not going to be able to remember any of this for long."

Years later I realized she had listened to me that day because I found tags on each item identifying the contents of the trunks. She also identified as many of the old pictures as she could and put them in albums. Beginning with the information she found in the trunks, she completed further research and eventually traced her family back to Ireland and Scotland. My father and brother later conducted a similar search for my father's family and traced it back to Scotland. As one of the more interesting parts of Mom's work on the trunks' contents, she removed for transcription and preservation one set of letters that was Civil War vintage. The Civil War letters in their protective binder were shelved, along with current books, in the family library. I looked at them sometimes and discussed them at school, but I never really thought about the people who wrote them and how they related to me as family. They were just another curious part of my family's past and my own childhood.

It also did not occur to me to wonder if more old letters existed other than the Civil War ones, at least not until years later when my father brought the trunk and its contents to me after my mother died. I then discovered more letters did exist - many, many more - yellowed with faded ink and some chewed by mice but still readable. Also, the old trunk contained ambrotype pictures that had never been identified, pictures I was later to learn, of the people who wrote the letters. Enthralled and captured, I listened to the voices in the letters. I thought I knew all of my mother's family because of the research she had done, but these people were new. I realized that I wanted to know these long ago people and how they related to me. Who were they? Where were these places with the unusual names? To find out, I began my own journey backward in time to 1861 when the earliest letter was written. The Civil War had just begun, and the Louisiana household of my great, great grandfather, William H. Jordan, was committed to the Confederate war effort. Born in Georgia and raised in Mississippi, his Southern blood ran deep, but he held his own views and went his own way. He had moved his family to Louisiana from Mississippi instead of staying with his father and inheriting his father's land. His father, Gray Jordan, also played a part in my journey. His voice was one of the voices from the Civil War letters, voices that had been locked in my memory bank since childhood.

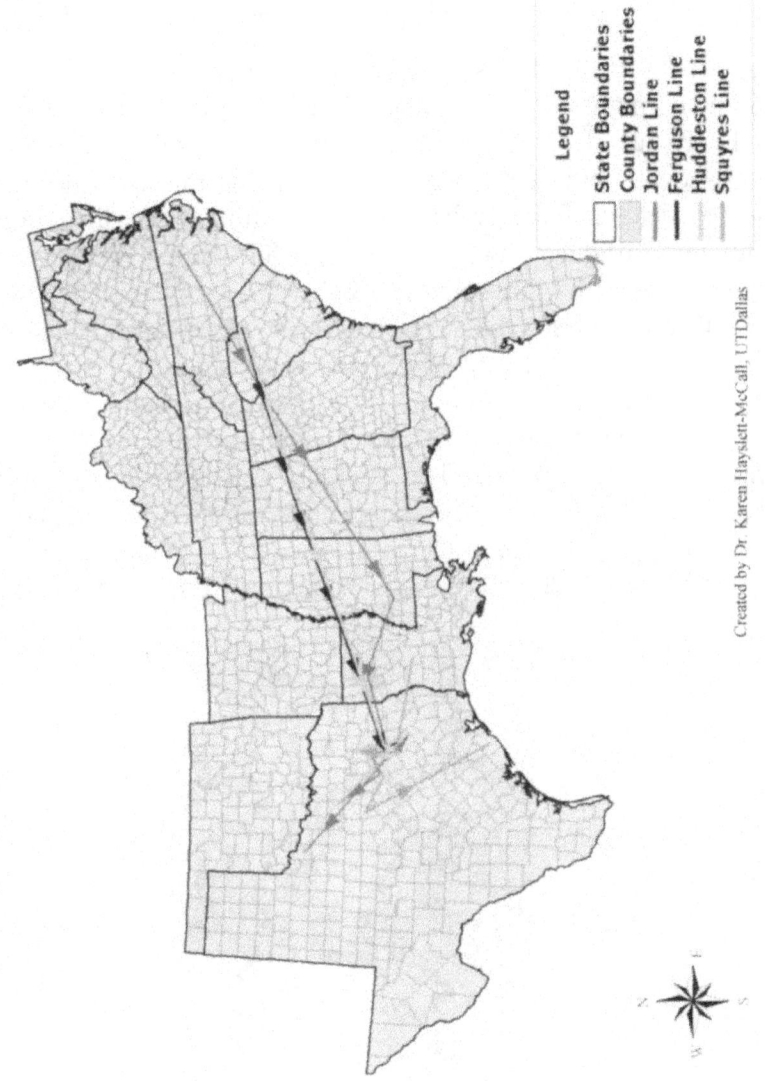

Family Emigration Across America

Legend

State Boundaries
County Boundaries
Jordan Line
Ferguson Line
Huddleston Line
Squyres Line

Created by Dr. Karen Hayslett-McCall, UTDallas

Chapter 2

As W.H. Jordan sat on his front porch on a hot, Louisiana summer's night in 1860, he looked out upon his land and saw what he had seen all of his life, trees and more trees, tall stately pines and sturdy oaks with dense undergrowth. In the midst of the forest lay cleared fields and pastureland. Heavy with moisture, the still air was thick and difficult to breathe. His skin felt damp. The forest rustled and chirped with night sounds. What was he contemplating? Perhaps he was remembering the back-breaking work it had taken to carve his homestead and fields out of the surrounding forest. Perhaps he was thinking of his family and how fine his children were growing up to be, or perhaps he was remembering his family back in Mississippi and his boyhood home. The land he was looking at was almost identical to his father's Mississippi farm, and the hot, humid air felt familiar as well.[1] Here in the stillness of the evening, he had time to remember his youth and where he had come from to get to this place.

William H. Jordan

William H. Jordan's father, Gray Jordan, was born in North Carolina on May 19, 1794.[2] He and Jordan family members and friends emigrated from North Carolina to Franklin Co., in northeastern Georgia, between 1800 and 1807. After the group had lived there for about ten years, Gray married William's mother, Margaret (Peggy) Chandler, the daughter of a family friend, on December 19, 1816, and William was born the next year on August 30, 1817.[3]

Sometime around 1818, the entire group of Jordans and friends, including Gray and his young family, moved on to Lawrence County, Mississippi,[4] possibly along the old Federal road which had been extended as far as Natchez, Mississippi by 1808.[5] A road in this part of America in 1818 was little better than an old Indian trail carved wide enough through the forest to allow a wagon to pass. When the rains came, the path turned into a sea of mud, becoming impassable to travelers in conveyances with wheels. How could the Jordan families and their friends travel these roads, look at the dense forests of southwestern Mississippi, and imagine homes, fields and pasture lands? It was simply a matter of seeing potential. What they were seeing when they looked upon this land was rich soil and plentiful water, and they were not afraid of the hard work it would take to establish farms because they knew that others who had come before them had been able to build in this place.[6]

When they arrived in Lawrence County, they found a land just recently vacated by the Choctaw Indian Nation. Perhaps the only reason the land was available at all to new settlers was because the Native Americans had moved on to other places or been removed by the United States government. A village of Choctaws had thrived in what would later become the Mt. Moriah Baptist Church Cemetery area, planting maize, wild rice, yams, and hills of herbs in the rich bottom land of the Bogue Chitto River. These Native Americans were gone by the time the Jordans arrived, but several of the families with which the Jordans became acquainted in their new home had arrived early enough to the area to have interaction with the Choctaws.[7] One of these families was the Hart family. This family in later years produced a daughter, Martha, who became William's wife.

In 1820 Lawrence County, Mississippi, was showing great promise of supporting a prosperous agrarian society. Hundreds of thousands of board feet of lumber had been removed from the forested areas to make room for homes, fields of cotton and other crops, pasture lands, and water mills for processing grain. The wealthier plantation owners in the county lived along the Pearl River because the land that lay in the flood plain of this major river contained rich soil. If the land owner could survive his land occasionally being flooded, he had fine soil for planting crops. The river also served as a highway for transporting crops to market by boat or barge and people to larger cities when necessary. Cotton was a major crop, but land owners also planted rice, sugar cane, and grains for livestock feed.[8] In spite of all the attractions of the Pearl River region, the Jordan families and their friends moved on past the Pearl to settle farther west in Lawrence County on a branch of the Bogue Chitto River, which they named Jordan Creek, a few miles south of the area which later became the town of Brookhaven, Mississippi. The reason for this may have been that the land along the Pearl had all been claimed by the time the Jordans arrived, but then again, maybe the Jordans just preferred the land farther west in the county. It is even possible that the Jordans knew others who had moved there from Georgia. The western lands provided rich soil, adequate drinking water from springs and streams, and plenty of available land. Mills for processing grain had already been built on some of the streams, and at least one semblance of a road ran beside the Bogue Chitto River.[9]

The Jordan families' land, when counted altogether, consisted of several thousand acres, but much of it was wooded and never cultivated. Fields and homesteads were carved out of the forests on the basically flat terrain. High humidity in the summer months meant only a little activity produced a sizable amount of perspiration. The back-breaking work of clearing the land, building homes, and planting fields must have produced a lot of it. As well, the occasional swamp-like conditions of the forests due to humidity, standing water, and insects probably contributed to the numerous cases of fever among the families of the region. For the first few years, the Jordans and their friends did not have slaves but more than likely shared the labor required to establish farms. In later years, some of the Jordans became slave owners but never on the scale of the large plantations.[10]

They had large families to provide most of the labor they needed to work the land.

In Gray Jordan's young family, William did not remain an only child for long. His sister Malinda was born in 1818, his brother, Wyatt, was born on February 10, 1819, followed by his brothers Samuel on November 22, 1821, and James on October 22, 1823.[11] The boys were too young to help their father carve his farm out of the forest, but as soon as they were old enough, they helped him maintain it and enlarge the pasture and tillable land. For the boys, growing up in the forest meant many opportunities for adventure in the guise of hunting, fishing, camping, and collecting all sorts of animal pets. Old Indian trails and relics such as arrowheads made for a boy's paradise. Now, in thinking about this time of growing up with his brothers, William remembered years of hard work but also, with a grin, many happy hours of play and mischief. He could still picture himself and his brothers, Wyatt, Samuel, and James as they dodged and scampered among the trees of the forest, becoming explorers, Indian scouts, Revolutionary soldiers and spies, limited only by their active imaginations. He was especially fond of Wyatt, the brother who was closest in age to him.

Jordan's Creek

In the years that followed 1823, Gray and Margaret added four girls to the family, Martha Ann on October 30, 1825, Susan around 1826, Mary Ann on August 25, 1832, and around 1838 a daughter whose name is currently unknown. Finally on February

18, 1840, another son was born, Simeon, the last child.[12] Life was good most of the time when everyone was healthy and busy working on the farm. The other families who had emigrated from Georgia, especially the Chandlers, lived in the neighborhood surrounding Jordan Creek, creating a large interwoven community with several families who had lived in the area before the Jordans arrived. This community of families hosted many gatherings of family and friends at social events. The children grew up together, playing, learning, and exploring the land. As the years went by, several of the children from each of the families married one another, bringing the families even closer.

As W.H. Jordan's memories continued that sultry night in 1860 Louisiana, he recalled his own marriage on October 18, 1838, to Martha Price and the beginning of his family. Martha was the daughter of Joseph and Mary Hart Price, who lived further south on the Bogue Chitto River and were early settlers of the county.

Martha Price Jordan

William and Martha's first son was born in 1840, Floyd H., followed by two daughters, Mary Elizabeth on June 22, 1841, and Margaret Jane on February 18, 1842. Two more boys were added to the family in the 1840s, James Monroe in 1845 and Pierre (Perry) Lafayette in 1849. Meanwhile, William's brother, Wyatt, married Martha McRorque (some records have McRosser) on January 24, 1844, and they had three children in the 1840s, Caroline on November 24, 1844, Julia Ann (Juliann) in 1846, and Wilson in 1849.[13] William and Wyatt and their families lived in the Jordan Creek area and other areas of Mississippi such as Meridian, until 1850 when they decided to move to Louisiana.[14] In making this move, William and Wyatt were turning away from their inheritance of Gray Jordan's estate, perhaps irrevocably. The reason for William's decision could have been a desire for independence or the lure of a new, attractive location, or simply his restless nature. However, it set a pattern for the rest of his life; a new and better place always waited just over the horizon. Wyatt followed his brother's lead because the two brothers were very close. What drew them to Louisiana?

Brush Valley in Bienville Parish, of northwestern Louisiana, was a land of red dirt considered excellent for raising cotton, and in 1850 the promise of the land must have attracted the Jordan brothers. Perhaps the land was even being advertised, because Hardy Jordan, a brother or cousin of Gray Jordan, decided to move his family to northern Louisiana around 1850 as well.[15] By 1860 the promise of the land had been fulfilled and Bienville Parish was very prosperous with cotton farmers and slave owners. However, in spite of the wishes of many citizens, the parish never reflected the genteel plantation culture of other parts of the state and the South.[16] Bienville Parish lacked the large river that was so advantageous for truly prosperous plantations, and this may have been the reason the plantation culture never fully developed in the area. Nevertheless, religious and educational institutions as well as local government services were well established by 1860,[17] and the Jordans were undoubtedly attracted to the parish, having come from another booming cotton region in Mississippi. The now Louisiana Jordans did not own large tracts of land and were not slave owners.[18] They could manage the farm operations themselves without an extra labor force, and their children were old enough to help.

The land was hilly, and it contained gravel and iron ore deposits as well as a wealth of pine and oak trees. If the land could be cleared of trees, the creek areas contained fine pastureland and soil for crops, especially cotton. The land and climate were very similar to what the Jordans had known in Mississippi, adding to the appeal of the place for them. The large salt deposits nearby at Winnfield were well known as far away as Mississippi. The sandy soil at Saline, a town not too far from the Jordan farm, was perfect for raising watermelons, and another neighboring town, Ruston, was known for its peaches.[19] William settled a few miles southwest of the town of Friendship, and Wyatt obtained land in two parcels, each about twenty miles from William.[20]

By 1854 William and Wyatt were busy building homes and farms in Louisiana, and in Mississippi, Gray and Margaret Jordan's other children were all married and/or gone from home except Simeon. One child, Malinda (married to John Robert Randall), had returned with her children to live at her parents' home after her husband died. Two of the Jordan children had also died, Susan and the currently unknown daughter. However, Susan had married James Chandler and had two children by him before her death. One of the Gray Jordans' children, Samuel, disappeared from family records, and nothing is known about him.[21] The remaining Jordan children in Mississippi had married well, started families, and were accumulating land of their own. James married Martha Chandler, Martha married Joseph Sutton, and Mary Ann married William Martin Hickman.[22]

The community around the Bogue Chitto River in Lawrence County, Mississippi, also grew and matured. When Gray and Margaret first arrived in the area, farms and plantations had to be virtually self-sufficient because no goods and services were available except through primitive trading posts. No market existed for excess grains and crops, and there was no viable means of transportation for getting the products to a market. This all changed with the coming of the Great Northern Railroad to the small hamlet of Brookhaven in 1856-57. Brookhaven grew into a town with services available for the outlying farms and plantations, and cotton and grain production boomed because of the railroad that could transport the crops to market. At last, a market was established for the timber that was cleared each year from the land in Lawrence County, and sawmills were built.[23] Slave ownership also grew, and Gray obtained a small group of slaves to help him farm because most of his children were gone.[24]

Unfortunately, in the midst of this successful economic and "empty nest" period, Gray and Margaret's marriage disintegrated. After almost forty years of living together, arguments, petty jealousies, imagined slights, and real verbal abuse had taken their toll and had made continuing with the marriage very difficult. Perhaps the Jordans' relative prosperity contributed to their problems because some of the disagreements centered around one of the female slaves owned by the Jordans. Charges and countercharges flew back and forth, filtered through the mouths of attorneys.

> The conduct of the defendant [Gray] towards the claimant [Margaret] has been harsh, cold, unfeeling, and at times cruel, he has apparently lost his wanted affection for her, has refused to furnish her with comfortable clothing and many indispensable conveniences, has been uniformly harsh in his language and gross and unfeeling in his conduct towards her, and has used every means, including actual force, to drive her from home until she has been forced to take up residence with a married daughter.[25]

> The defendant [Gray] denies that he ever was guilty or encouraged or connived at any cruelty or harsh usage towards the claimant [Margaret], and avers that so far as any war of words may have happened or extended between them it was provoked, instigated and continued by the claimant herself, prompted either by an original bad and ungovernable temper or excited by other ridiculous and unfounded motives which the claimant understands and which the defendant cannot go into in his response to the charges. The claimant left of her own accord his house, when he was not at home, vowing she would never return and would have accepted his proposed settlement except that she wished to run him to as much expense and cost as possible.[26]

Only family members knew which party was telling the truth, but more than likely some truth existed on both sides. The bitter end result became a matter of public record. Both parties mutually agreed to a divorce, and although it probably rocked the community at that time, the divorce was finalized in 1854. Margaret received three hundred and fifty dollars as a final settlement from Gray and lived with one of her married daughters, at least for a short period.[27] Gray married again to a much younger woman who had been married twice before and had four children of her own, Nancy Hickman Wallace Brister. Together they had three more children, Gray Jr. in April of 1857, Wilson in 1860, and Sarah in 1862.[28] The circumstances surrounding Gray Jr.'s birth are unclear according to his descendants because he was born in Arkansas while Nancy was there by herself being treated for diabetes or Bright's Disease as it was known then. She was not pregnant when she left home to go to Arkansas. For most of his life, Gray Jr.'s nickname was "Tap" which referred to the treatments his mother underwent in Arkansas. The treatments consisted of tapping or bleeding the patient. In spite of all this, Gray Sr. accepted Gray Jr. as his son.[29]

William Jordan's recollections of his Mississippi family that Louisiana night in 1860 must have included the problems in his parent's marriage, and perhaps these problems were one of the reasons for his move away from Mississippi. Switching his thoughts to a more cheerful subject, his own marriage in the 1850s was solid and had produced more children, Martha in 1852 and William C. on December 3, 1855. His brother Wyatt had been similarly blessed with four new children in this time period, Ellen (Emily) in 1851, Simon in 1854, Isaac in 1856, and Andrew in 1859. (An eighth and final child, Tabitha, would be born later in 1861.)[30] The 1850s in Louisiana had been good years for the Jordans' with growing families, productive farms, and close family and community ties. The brothers and their wives had gotten together often to work on each other's farms, to celebrate some special occasion, or just to visit, while the cousins in the families had grown up together, attending school, church, and parties. School and church activities had provided opportunities for the Jordans to make friends with other families in the area, creating a close, supportive community of people. There had even been a wedding in the William Jordan family in June of 1860. The first of William and Martha's children to wed, their daughter, Mary Elizabeth (Lizzie), had married George Bates on June 20, 1860.[31]

Because life was so good, William Jordan was content that night in 1860, thinking of his wife, his fine young sons and daughters, his land, and the bright future ahead in Brush Valley with his friends and neighbors. He had stayed ten years in one place and had built a life there that he enjoyed. There was no reason for him to think of moving on at this point. However, change was already in the wind, and it was not to be a good change. The talk of civil war must also have crept into his thoughts that night.

Jordan Family
Places of Interest
1820-1864

Mississippi

. Shreveport   . Ruston   . Monroe

. Liberty Hill
(Brush Valley)   Vicksburg .
. Saline

                                                        *Jackson   .
                                                                Meridian

. Mansfield   . Winnfield
. Pleasant Hill

                    Natchez .   . Brookhaven
. Natchitoches   . Monticello

.
Alexandria   Hattiesburg

                        Tangipahoa .
                        (Camp Moore)

Louisiana   * . Baton Rouge   Biloxi .

                                    . New Orleans

N

( ) Places, not towns or cities

Chapter 3

The good life that showed such promise for the Jordans in Brush Valley, Louisiana, came to a crashing end in 1861 when the American Civil War began with the conflict at Ft. Sumter, South Carolina. One by one, the Southern states, including Mississippi and Louisiana, seceded from the United States, forming the Confederate States of America. In spite of this upheaval, the Jordan family, like many others, first felt the war's impact personally with the new Confederate army's recruitment of soldiers. The recruitment did not attract William perhaps because he felt he was too old, because he felt his responsibilities lay at home, or because of reasons known only to himself. Initially, enlisting in the army did not appeal to Wyatt either. William and Wyatt's younger brothers and cousins in Mississippi, however, enlisted one after another through the early war years as did their cousins and second cousins in Louisiana. William's younger brother, James, was among the first Jordans to enlist in Mississippi.

Wyatt's children were too young to enlist, but William's were not. His oldest son, Floyd, was the first in the family to answer the new army's call from Bienville Parish, Louisiana. At twenty-one years old and unmarried, Floyd was perfect soldier material. He had already proven himself to be responsible and a hard worker, and he also had a sense of humor to give him some perspective. He came by this naturally as all of the Jordans knew how to tease and how to laugh. His unit was Company H, 9th Louisiana Infantry, and he was mustered into the Confederate army on June 29, 1861, at Camp Moore, Louisiana, with the rank of private.[1] Although they did not realize it at the time, the William Jordan family would never be the same again, nor would their world. Floyd wrote home from Camp Moore:

June 30, 1861
State of Louisiana
Parish of St. Helena
Dear Father and Mother,

I take my pen in hand to drop you a few lines to let you know that I am in camp now. We was mustered into service yesterday. I have been puny [sick] ever since I left home, but feel better now. There is not much sickness here now, but some of the boys have got the measles. I have got a good group of men and will tell you their names. Absolom Lord, Bunyan Prothro, James Holman, John Bradley, Henry Babers, Edward Ross, George Boyleston.

We landed here yesterday morning. They say there is twenty-eight hundred soldiers here now. We do not know when we will be sent out but some think that we will stay here about six months but we may leave this week. We were treated very well as we came out here. The people in Vernon gave us a big dinner as we came through and when we got to Monroe they offered to give us a flag but we could not wait for it. I want you to write to me as soon as you can. Tell all the family to write to me. What I write to one must answer for all of you. You must write your letters to St. Helena's Parish, Tangipaho P.O., Louisiana.

F.H. Jordan

I will start my ambrotype [picture] with this letter and I want you to let me know whether you get it or not.

As the letter relates, enthusiasm for the war was running high in the South in 1861, and many men were volunteering for the army. People were in a celebratory mood, cheering on the troops and making flags. The excitement was contagious, pervasive, and unfortunately very unrealistic. Although Floyd was enthusiastic and determined to be a good soldier at this point, he and the boys from his neighborhood were already beginning to experience one of the most discouraging aspects of the war, something which had nothing to do with glory and fighting but was every bit as deadly – disease. The realities of war in the 19th century were making themselves known even this early.

Floyd H. Jordan

At the beginning of the Civil War, Camp Moore, Tangipahoa, Louisiana, where Floyd was mustered into the army, quickly became a large staging and training area for the Louisiana Confederate troops. As many as six thousand men were assembled at the camp at any one time, learning close order drill, the army's intricate tactical movements of warfare on the battlefield. Located about seventy-eight miles north of New Orleans, the camp possessed favorable conditions for billeting and training large numbers of men, and the adjacent railroad was convenient for shipping the men out to other Southern states.[2] Coincidentally, Camp Moore was located only about sixty miles south of Brookhaven, Mississippi, where Floyd had been born.

When Floyd arrived, he saw the camp bounded on the west by the railroad, the south by Beaver Creek, and the east by the Tangipahoa River. Along the creek were located a coffee house and restaurant, a grocery, soda and refreshment shops, a barber shop, a photographer, and a butcher shop, all places to spend money if a soldier had any to spend. As described in Floyd's letter home of June 30, 1861, he did at least visit the photographer. The camp's center was the parade ground, flanked on the north and south by tent rows and on the east by a cemetery where, already, disease victims were being buried. Tent life could be made more bearable by the addition of a wood plank floor, an asset when the rains descended. Beaver Creek extended along the entire camp's length on the south and was the main water source for the camp. The soldiers' using it for laundry, bathing, and as a source of drinking water may have contributed to the disease problem although the drinking water area was upstream from the bathing/laundry area. Once companies were brought to full strength and formed into regiments, they were shipped out on the railroad.[3] In less than a month Floyd's regiment, the 9th Louisiana Infantry, was ready to go, its destination the Army of Northern Virginia at Richmond, Virginia.

State of Louisiana
Camp Moore
July 19, 1861
Dear Father,

I take my pen in hand to drop you a few lines to let you know that I am well at this time but I have been very sick with the flux [bloody dysentery] but if I keep mending like I have for the last day or two I will be as stout as ever.

All of our boys have been sick but they are all up again. I wrote to George [Bates, brother-in-law] that Absolom Lord had the measles but it was a mistake. It was just the fever.

I will tell you that a soldier has a hard time. Tell Mother and Margaret [sister] that I missed them very much today when I went to wash my clothes. Yesterday I had to cook. Me and Absolom Lord cooked together and it was very well done. I think that I would be satisfied if I could get to see my sweetheart, but I am a long way off from you all now, but I will soon be a heap further. We are going to start to Richmond, Virginia, in two or three days. I have wrote you one letter and sent it off, but I thought as long as I had the chance of sending it by hand, I would write to you again. I want you all to think of me when you go to eat watermelons and peaches. Tell Mother to send me the biggest watermelon she can find in a letter.

I must come to a close by signing my name for the drum is beating now.

F.H. Jordan

Camp Moore Parade Ground

For Floyd, homesickness was beginning to set in as he wrote about watermelons and peaches which were so easily obtained at home in July but hard to find at Camp Moore, his mother's cooking, her ability as a laundress, and an absent sweetheart, but worse than homesickness were the continued bouts with illness. Families in the 1860s South were frequently sick with fevers, influenza, malaria, and typhoid, because the swamp-like conditions of many areas included insects, heat, and humidity which all took their toll on people's health. Sanitary living, careful water and food preservation, and even proper diet were unheard of for most people. When the war began, large masses of men were removed from their usual environments and forced to live outside, enduring the elements in camps with little or no protection or sanitation. They were exposed to diseases that they probably would not have encountered at home, and this was especially true for men from rural environments like Floyd and his friends.[4] It is no wonder that disease ran rampant. During Floyd's stay at Camp Moore, a measles epidemic broke out which sent many young soldiers to the cemetery.[5] Many others shipped out carrying the germs of the disease to their next destination. Such was the case with Floyd's company.[6]

In the final Civil War casualty accounting, twice as many men died of disease as died in battle. More than 995 out of 1000 men eventually contracted chronic dysentery, typhoid fever caused one quarter of the non-combat deaths, malaria struck one quarter of all soldiers, pneumonia and tuberculosis accounted for at least half of the non-combat deaths, and contagious diseases such as mumps, measles, whooping cough, and chicken pox struck with a vengeance. Little was known about disease or antiseptic surgical techniques.[7] A great mass of men, including Floyd Jordan and his friends, had joined the army to fight the Yankees but found themselves in an entirely different kind of fight. They had to somehow remain healthy and on their feet if they were going to participate in any battles.

The 9th Louisiana Infantry arrived at Richmond too late to be involved in the first battle of Manassas (sometimes known as Bull Run) in 1861, but they participated in every Army of Northern Virginia campaign thereafter until the war's end, eventually being commanded by General Robert E. Lee.[8] Having missed First Manassas, the 9th could only wait until the next engagement. Coincidentally, the land on which the battle of First Manassas or Bull Run was fought had belonged to the Crume family more than fifty years before and a Crume descendant married Floyd Jordan's niece long after the Civil War was over.

Richmond, Virginia
August 6, 1861
Dear Sister,

I take my pen in hand to drop you a few lines, but I can't say to you that I am well. I have had the measles. I taken them the day after we landed here, and our company was called out the same day. And they left me and ten more of the boys here in camp, and we were taken to the hospital [Hospital of the Medical College of Virginia at Richmond, Virginia]. John Bradley and William Bradley and Davison Malone all died there. I came out of there four days ago. I was going to start to Manassas to my company, but the lady of this town told them I was too weak to go yet, that it would cause me to relapse again, and they said they would take care of me here. They got a house and put me and several other boys in it. I expect that we will stay here several days. The ladies here treat us very kind. They invite us out to eat with them, and when they don't invite us out, they send our provisions to us. We find a great many friends here.

They have been fighting very heavy at Manassas. We whipped them very bad. Last Sunday two weeks ago they fought the largest battle at Manassas that ever was fought. The Yankees killed and wounded 1500 of our men, while ours killed 25,000 of their men. They are fixing to fight there again. Every day I am in hopes that I will be with them the next time.

I have nothing more of importance to say at this time. You must not think hard of me for not writing to you all, for I have a bad chance to write. You must make one letter do you all. It is thought that the war will not last long, and I am in hopes that will be the case. If the Lord spares me life, I am in hopes that I will see you all soon. Tell Simon Shively and Angelina and all the rest of the neighbors that they must not think hard of me for not writing to them for I have had a bad chance to write. Tell Andrew Bishop that he must take good care of all the corn he has to spare. If I do not get back, maybe some of the rest will. Tell Mother that I have got me another mother, or she tends to me like a mother, but she is not half so near to me.

I have never heard from you all since I left you. I would like to hear from you, and would like much better to see you all. I must come to a close by signing my name.

Floyd H. Jordan

With this letter, Floyd's frustration with being ill and not being able to participate in the fighting was growing. He had contracted measles in the epidemic at Camp Moore in Louisiana, but it had not struck until he reached Virginia. It was a miracle that the whole company did not come down with it. However, apparently only eleven members of the company were infected, and Floyd was fortunate to receive some good care from the local citizenry that contributed to his recovery. For this his family was grateful when they finally received news of it. Other soldiers and their families were not so fortunate. Civilian support was vital to the Confederate armies, and this would become more apparent as the war stretched out over the years.

Floyd was also worried about conditions at home and

whether he was being missed. Encouraged by the early successes of the Confederate armies, Floyd, like many other Southern soldiers, hoped the war would be a short one. He would perform his duty, get the war over, and return home to life as usual. He was hoping that life at home would not go on without him while he was gone, depriving him of the opportunity for important things such as sweethearts and raising his beloved horses. His report of the Manassas casualty count revealed the Confederate optimistic view. Casualty figures were hard to determine by the common soldier during the chaos of battle and were probably inflated or deflated to positively affect soldier morale. However, even without exaggeration, the official number of casualties was very high in the major battles of the Civil War.

Of all his sisters, the sister that he wrote to from the battlefields of Virginia was Margaret Jane, age nineteen, and this was primarily because she was his best source of information about the neighborhood girls. He could hardly ask his parents about such things. Margaret, in turn, wanted to know about the boys from Brush Valley in her brother's company. They loved to tease each other because they shared the same sense of humor, but the information they exchanged was important too. Floyd trusted Margaret to get him the news he wanted and to be discreet about it.

Floyd's family must have been very worried about his continuing illness. He had drifted from one disease into another and even had to be hospitalized in Virginia. The wait for news concerning Floyd was torturous with the unreliability of the mail system. In Virginia, Floyd had difficulty getting his mail from home as well because he was constantly moving. Because of this worrisome situation, the family at home, although gravely concerned about Floyd's health, was probably still not fully aware of the serious nature of his peril. At this point, the South seemed to be handily winning the war.

June 30 1861
State of Louisiana
Parish of ~~Morvile~~ Athens
Dear father and
Mother I take my pen
in hand to drop you
a few lines to let you
no that I am in camps
we was Mustered in to
sarvis yesterday I have ben
puney ever sins I left
home but I feel better now
they is not much sickness
hear now but some of
the boys has got the
mazels I have got a very
good mes and I will tel
you their names Absalom
Earl James Hardaman
Henry Bakers ~~Fartin~~
Gorge Bailstow Burson
Brother John Bradly
Edward Ross

we landed hear yesterday
Morning they say they is
twenty Eight hundred
soalders hear now we do not
no when we will be sent
off but some some thinks
that we will stay hear
about six months but
we may leave this weak
we was trated very well
as we came out hear they
peaple in virnen gave
us a big dinner as we came
through and when we
got to Monro they
ladys offerd to give us
a blag but we coul
not wait for it I wont
you to rych to me
as soo as I cam tell
the the of the family
to rychl to me

what if I right.
to one must answer
for all of you
you get best right
your letters to
St Hellena Parish. Tangipaho Post
office Louisiana
H. H. Jordan
I will start
my ambrotipe
with this letter
and I won you
to let me no
whether you get it
or not.

Chapter 4

After recovering somewhat from his illnesses, Floyd Jordan finally returned to his company which was still camped in the Manassas, Virginia, vicinity. In his letters home, he repeated the same stories because he was never sure that a letter would reach its destination. Mail delivery was highly uncertain during the war, and when he had the chance to send a letter with a soldier who was returning home, he took it, even if it meant repeating the same pieces of news again that he had already written home in other letters. The movement of troops interfered with mail delivery; moreover, soldiers who became separated from their regular companies due to illness, injury, or transfer were often cut off from their mail. Mail was also lost or captured by enemy troops or destroyed in battle. For all these reasons, letters were precious indeed to their recipients. Floyd was having trouble receiving letters as well as sending them out, and most of his letters complained about this even though it did no good.

Camp Bienville, Virginia
August 30, 1861
Dear Father,

I take my pen in hand to drop you a few lines, hoping you are all well. I am not right well myself. I left Richmond a week ago and came to Manassas to my company, and I taken a very bad cold. There is a great deal of sickness in camp now. There is not many dangerous cases in camps now. There has been several deaths in our company. George Boyleston died the night before last. Andrew Prat is dead and Ben Howard and several others. The most of the boys that came out of that neighborhood is able for service. James Holman, Furman Babers, Henry Burk and Jesse Raborn are sick, but they are all able to be up.

I have been very sick since I saw you last. I took the measles as soon as we got to Richmond, and our regiment was ordered to come to Manassas and I was left in the tent. I stayed there three days, and then I was hauled to the hospital. I stayed in there ten days, and I got a discharge, and I came out and took sick again. And then I stayed in a private house where I was treated as well as if I had been at home. I had anything I wanted to eat and a good bed to sleep on and all the good attention that I could wish for. And when I went to leave there, the lady I was staying with gave me two good flannel shirts and told me that if I got sick or wounded to come back and she would take care of me until I got well. But I am about 150 miles from there now, and that much further from home.

There has been a right smart of fighting done here, but our men didn't get here in time to be in the battle. They got here the day after the battle. They say that it was the largest battle that ever was known. There has been fighting at Falls Church in Virginia, and the South whipped them, but I have not heard how many they killed.

I have nothing of importance to write at this time. I want you to write to me once a week, but you will have to make a better start than what you are doing at the present if you do for I have never got but one letter since I left home.

George [Bates, brother-in-law], give my respects to all my friends and tell them to write to me. Direct your letters to Manassas Junction, Virginia.

F.H. Jordan
To W.H. Jordan

P.S. I also hear that Darling Babers was very bad off at Richmond.

After the first battle of Manassas, which the 9th Louisiana Infantry, part of the 1st Louisiana Brigade, had missed, Floyd's unit continued to stay in the Manassas area with other units of the Army of Northern Virginia. The one skirmish at Falls Church did not escalate into a major battle, and the Confederate troops had orders to hold their position and not advance. By the fall of 1861, Floyd had begun to receive some mail from home, but the weather was beginning to turn cold, much colder that he was used to back home in Louisiana. He realized he was going to need warmer clothing, and he was hoping to receive some from home. He had still not been in a battle. He was losing more friends and acquaintances to death from disease than from fighting, and his own health continued to be unsteady with periods of illness.

Floyd was an example of what happened when large numbers of men were held in one position for an extended period. The longer they stayed in one place in the outdoor camps, the more sanitary conditions deteriorated and the likelihood grew that the troops would fall ill. This same scenario happened over and over again during the war. The men seldom developed any resistance to the diseases prevalent in the camps, and the inadequate sanitation insured illness would strike without end.[1] Soon winter weather would add to the misery. As Floyd recounted in his letter, the roll call of the neighborhood boys included names of the sick, the very sick, and the dead. Only a few months earlier, Floyd was listing these same boys as new, enthusiastic soldiers in the Confederate Army, young and full of life.

Camp Bienville, Virginia
October 4, 1861
Dear sister,

I take my pen in hand to answer your kind letters. I received three letters from you. One was wrote August the 15th, one September the 9th, and one September 15th. I would have wrote to you a heap sooner if I could have mailed my letters, but we have been moving. We only moved two miles. A part of our brigade went on to the Potomac and met the Yankees, but they would not fight. They met to have battle, but the Yankees run, and our men fired on them and killed three of them.

You wrote to me that there was a young lady there that wanted to see me, but you did not tell me her name, but you must the next letter you write to me. You wrote to me that Mother was going to send me some clothes the next week. I would be very glad to get them, for it is very cold country here, so the people say that live here. We have just been given a good suit of clothes and twenty dollars in money.

Tell Mother I would like to get a letter from her. I want you all to write as often as you can. You must not wait for me to answer your letters for I have a bad chance to mail my letters.

I would like to hear from you all every day or two, but I had rather see you all. I hope the Lord will be with me and help me to return home again.

If I never meet you on Earth again, I hope I will meet you in Heaven. So nothing more at present.

F.H. Jordan
To Margaret Jordan

Margaret Jane Jordan

Floyd wrote the following letter the next day, hoping at least one letter would get through to his family. He had been sick again. Although his family was used to illness, they must have been worried about his failure to gain strength and remain healthy. The serious bout with the measles had weakened his resistance, and living outdoors once again, he caught a cold. On the other hand, during this early part of the Civil War, Southern soldiers were at least provisioned fairly well. They were issued clothes and money. As for entertainment, the mail was just about the only entertainment a soldier had unless he wanted to gamble on card games or partake of the pleasures of the camp followers.[2] Therefore Floyd continued to ask for more letters, even though his family and friends were writing to him on a fairly regular basis. All of the Jordans could read and write, even the women, so letter writing was a common activity, and it was the only way for families in 1860 to communicate with relatives who lived far away. The boredom in between fighting engagements also lay heavily upon Floyd; he had very little to do except try to take care of himself in less than favorable conditions. Getting leave to go into a nearby town didn't happen very often.[3] Writing letters helped a little, and receiving letters from home with enticing comments in them about neighborhood girls who were inquiring about him helped even more.

Camp Bienville, Virginia
October 5th A.D. 1861
Dear Father and Mother,

I seat myself this morning to let you know that I am tolerably well at this time. I have had a spell of the fever which lasted me about two weeks, but I am mending very fast now. I received your send about ten days ago, which I read with great pleasure, but I would be glad if you would write oftener than you do. You wrote to me that you wanted me to get a razor strap to Lincoln's back, but I think that would be too mean to treat a good man's dog, although Lincoln, I expect, is a very mean man, but I hope he will change, and if he don't, we will make him change if we can get to him.

Our brigade has moved on to the Potomac. They got after the Yankees the other day, but they would not fight. When they started to run, our men fired on them and killed three of them, but they run across the Potomac and our men couldn't get to them.

I have not been in a fight yet. I was glad to hear that my filly was doing well. I want you to write soon and tell me how much corn and cotton you have made. You must not think hard of me for not writing to you sooner, for I had a bad chance to mail my letters. Give my respects to Uncle Wyatt and family and all of my friends. So nothing more at present, only I remain

Your affectionate son until death,
F.H. Jordan

The politics of the Civil War received some mention for the first time in this letter. Obviously William and Martha Jordan, Floyd's parents, did not like President Lincoln. They were staunch Southerners, and, like many Southerners, they placed a lot of the blame for the war on Lincoln's shoulders. His inability to compromise with the Southern concerns about states' rights and slavery made him seem mean and unreasoning. He became the focal point for Southern hatred. Floyd's parents probably did not hate Lincoln because it was not in their nature to hate anyone, but they blamed him for the war that was imperiling their family. Floyd seemed to take a humorous attitude towards this and his parents probably did too at times, but he was deadly serious about being a soldier or he would not have been where he was, far from home and ready to come under enemy fire. The close of all his letters home revealed not only the letter writing conventions of his time but also his preoccupation with thoughts of his own demise. Even though he had yet to be involved in any serious fighting, he, like his fellow soldiers, must have felt that death was a constant companion.

In this letter Floyd mentioned the crops that his family normally raised in Louisiana, his horse, and his friends and neighbors. Floyd hungered to hear about ordinary life at home, not only because these activities were the concerns of his normal life and the things that he was missing, but also because hearing about life at home kept him centered on who he really was in the surreal surroundings in which he found himself with the war. Because he was far from home and living under poor conditions, sick most of the time, and bored the rest of the time, it would have been easy for him to forget who he was, where his home was, and why he was fighting in a war. The letters from home served to remind him of all these things and were his lifeline to sanity. They also brought him close to his loved ones who were his support system and so very far away. He couldn't receive enough letters.

Jordan Civil War Sites
Hospitals, Camps, and Battlefields
1861-1862

( ) Places but not towns or cities.

Sharpsburg, Md.

Frederick, Md.

Centerville Falls Church

Alexandria

Washington D.C.

Manassas

(Camp Bienville)

Harper's Ferry

(Bunker Hill)

Winchester

Front Royal

(Camp Brag)

(Cedar Mountain)

Orange

Gordonsville

(Malvern Hill)

Richmond

(Cold Harbor)

(Cross Keys)

Port Republic

Charlottesville

Virginia

Farmville

(Camp Girondelet)

Lynchburg

Danville

N

Chapter 5

During the last months of 1861 and the early months of 1862, Floyd Jordan continued to be ill, and this included a visit to the General Hospital #1 at Danville, Virginia, where he was treated and then transferred to the Orange Courthouse Hospital in Orange County.[1] No letters survived from this period, so nothing is known about Floyd's participation or lack thereof in battle. This was probably an inactive period for his company because the company's military record does not show any engagements with the enemy until May 23, 1862.[2] He was remustered into the Confederate army on February 11, 1862, for the duration of the war, and after release from the hospital at Farmville, Virginia, he returned to his company at Camp Carondelet.[3]

On March 12, 1862, two more Jordans from Louisiana entered the war and joined Company H of the 9th Louisiana Infantry in Virginia. James Monroe, Floyd's seventeen-year-old younger brother, and his Uncle Wyatt enlisted.[4] Wyatt was 43 years old in 1862 and leaving behind a wife and eight children, four of whom were under ten years old. George Bates, husband of William Jordan's daughter Mary Elizabeth (Lizzie), also joined the army at this time and came with the rest to Virginia.[5] The war was not going to end quickly as had earlier been thought, and every man was needed. One can almost imagine the arguments that resounded between the two brothers, William and Wyatt, before Wyatt enlisted.

"Are you out of your mind?" roared William. "You aren't a kid playin' in the forest and campin' out anymore. You're used to a comfortable bed and clean livin' conditions. You cain't hope to keep up with those young bucks in the army."

"I'm not that old and slow, and I'm still the best shot in the family. I'll git used to campin' out agin right quick," calmly replied Wyatt.

"What about Martha and the kids? If somethin' happens to

you, what will they do?"

"That's what you're there for, big brother. And besides, Wilson is a good helper now."

"Wilson is twelve years old, hardly a substitute for you. You've got four kids under ten years old, includin' a new baby. What can I say to talk you out of this?" reasoned William.

"Nothin'," replied Wyatt. "The South needs every man it can git. Unlike those other fools, I don't think this war will be over quick. I need to do what I can to help, and I need to know that you're here to take care of my family if need be. Can I count on you?"

"You know you can," rejoined William, punching his brother's arm. "But you're a damned fool, an old one at that!"

"Maybe," Wyatt punched his brother back. "But I have to do this."

James Monroe Jordan

State of Virginia
Camp Brag
May the 7th, 1862
Dear Mother,

    I take my pen in hand to drop you a few lines to let you

know that I am well. George [Bates] is in good health at present. We were on a march and Floyd was puny [sickly] so he went down to the hospital. This is the sixth march that we have made since we got here. They have had several fights around us. I am hearing the cannons at this time. I was on picket one morning, and I saw the cannons firing from both sides. I could see the bombs bursting about the timbers.

You must take good care of Sealom [his horse] and make him grow fast. When we were starting on a march, we sent our clothes on the cart, and we have not heard from them. I don't expect to ever see them again. We get plenty flour, beef, and bacon to eat. I have heard from Floyd and he was getting along mighty well at that time.

I have heard that New Orleans was taken by the Yankees. I have seen many a curiosity since I saw you. I must come to a close. I have nothing more to write at this time. Excuse my short letter. So I remain your affectionate son until death. So I send my love and best respects to all my inquiring friends.

To Martha L. Jordan
James M. Jordan

James, at seventeen, wrote a different kind of letter from his older, steadier brother, more descriptive of the things he was seeing and experiencing, even the food he was eating. This last was probably because his mother would want to know if he was eating enough and what he was eating. Excited to be in the war because it was a great adventure to him, he could have cared less about unimportant things such as clothes. However, he may have mentioned his lost clothes in order to send a subtle hint to the folks back home to send more. He also sent news of others from home who were in close proximity to him, and Floyd did this as well. He, like his brother, was concerned about how things were at home. The fall of New Orleans was a source of worry, but more important was the welfare of his horse. He was seventeen and in the middle of the greatest adventure of his life. The fall of New Orleans meant more to his parents who could see that everything was not going smoothly for the South in the war. James also wrote to his sister, Margaret.

Camp Brag, Virginia
May the 9th 1862
Dear Sister,

I take my pen in hand to drop you a few lines to let you know that I am well at this time. Floyd and George are well. There is a right smart of sickness in camp. Uncle Wyatt is sent to the hospital. He had the mumps. Times are very late, but the people are just fixing to plant. Some of the trees are just beginning to put out their blooms. W.O. Bates is sent to the hospital and H. [Henry] Babers.

Tell all the girls that I send my love and best wishes to them. I have not done anything yet. I sent my clothes on when we started on a march, and I have not heard from them yet, and I don't ever expect to. Tell Lizabeth to tell the folks howdy for me. Tell Granville Whitcomb and Chris to write to me. Tell Mother that I sent my ambrotype [picture] to her. George did not send his. I want you to write to me. I have not heard from home yet. There has not been but one letter received in this company yet. Billy Upshane got one. It was sent by hand to him. I heard that Sam Chestnut was dead. He taken the measles and was sent to the hospital. I have nothing of importance. You must excuse my short letter. I must come to a close. I hope these few lines may find you all well. So I remain your affectionate brother until death.

This to Margaret J. Jordan.

J.M. Jordan

Perry [younger brother], I want you to take good care of Sealom [James's horse] and make him grow fast, and I will pay you when I get back, but you must not ride him.

The Jordans and the other men in their company had yet to see battle. They had endured long marches, boredom, and disease but no fighting. Their friends and acquaintances were dying, but not from engagements with the enemy. Several, including Floyd and Wyatt, were in and out of the hospital with various illnesses. With no fighting to occupy his time, James, like his brother Floyd, was beginning to wonder if he was missing out on some things at home. He commented upon the difference between the Louisiana and Virginia planting seasons, an indication that he was thinking about what was happening in Brush Valley. As with Floyd, his sister Margaret Jane, was James's source of information about the neighborhood girls back in Bienville Parish. James also asked about his friends. At home, James had his twelve-year-old brother Perry taking care of his horse for a price. Perry was obviously an enterprising young man, aware of his opportunities. However, James did not extend his generosity to letting his younger brother ride the horse. Meanwhile, older brother Floyd had been keeping an eye on the new recruits from his family.

Camp Brag, Virginia
May 11th 1862
Dear Sister,

I take my pen in hand to drop you a few lines to let you know that I am well at this time, hoping these few lines may come safe to hand and find you all enjoying the same blessing. Monroe [James] and George both are well. Uncle Wyatt is at the hospital, but I hope that he will be able to come to camp soon. We have lost one man since we got back. Sam Chestnut died a few days ago. I have nothing of importance to write at this time. I wrote to Father a few days ago, but I have the chance to send this letter to Sparta by hand, and I thought I would write again for fear that you did not get the other letters that I wrote to you. This is the second letter that I have wrote to you since I got back [to camp] and the same to Father and Mother, but I have not received any answer. It is not worthwhile to say anything about the rest of the boys, for I wrote all about them the other day. You are too anxious to hear anything about them anyhow.

I want you to write to me all you know about the girls. I would like to hear from you very much. Tell Mother that Monroe [James] is a splendid cook. My excuse for bad writing is that I stood guard yesterday and last night. Give my best respects to all of the relations and friends and to Miss "You Know Who." So nothing more at present, only I remain your affectionate brother until death.

F.H. Jordan

Here Floyd indicated a general interest in the girls back

home and perhaps one special one. As a gentle way of teasing his sister, he also declined to say anything further about the men in his company, not only because he had already discussed them in another letter, but because his sister was either too worried about them or she was too eager to hear about them. Floyd's letters often displayed his ready sense of humor, as evidenced by the comment about his brother being a good cook. His health seemed to be improving at this time, but his Uncle Wyatt was not so fortunate.

In May, shortly after he arrived in Virginia, Wyatt Jordan went to the hospital at Charlottesville, Virginia, with a case of the mumps. It was a serious disease for an older man, and even though he was in a hospital and receiving care, little was known about treating the disease. Wyatt was unable to combat it, perhaps because his resistance had already been weakened by living outdoors in poor conditions. On May 17, 1862, he died. The official cause of death was listed as pneumonia in his military records.[6] He had been in the war for a little more than two months and never fired a shot in battle. His desire to serve his country because soldiers were badly needed would now not come to fruition because of a disease he never would have envisioned affecting him. Wyatt left behind eight children for his wife to raise alone. He was buried at the Soldiers Cemetery at the University of Virginia at Charlottesville.[7] William's worst fears had been realized, and there was nothing that he could do except inform his father and the family in Mississippi of the senseless loss. Gray Jordan referred to this in his letter to William in 1862.

Lawrence Co., Mississippi
July the 27th, 1862
Dear Son,

I seat myself to drop you a few lines to let you know that my family is not very well at this time, but is on the mend. We have had the fever but are on the mend at this time. I was glad to hear from you all once more in life. I was sorry to hear that news about your brother [Wyatt]. I want you to write to me whether it is sorrow or not in your next letter. Dear son, you said that you had written to me and hadn't had no answer, but I had written to you since I had a answer. I thought the mail was all done away with.

Your brother Sime [Simeon] is in the army. I heard from him a few days ago - is not very well at this time. Your brother James has got a final discharge from being a cripple. Dear son, I can say that the prospect for crops is tolerable bad for we haven't had rain. I think that if we get rain in a few days that we will make enough to make out on. Everything is high and scarce here, salt especially. I think if my health will permit, I will come over this fall to see you all and get some salt.

Dear son, I think that our country is in a bad fix. I don't know what will become of the widows and children that is left alone here for all the men is gone. Dear son, your sister [Mary Ann] and family is not well and is not been well all the summer. She is a widow. Mr. Hickmond [William Martin Hickmon] is dead.

Dear son, I haven't anything to interest you. I want you to write me when you get this. Dear son, I must say something about my little children. I have three of the smartest that you ever saw, two sons and one daughter [Gray, Wilson, and Sarah]. I must close my letter. Give my love to all of my friends and accept a due portion for yourself. Good-bye dear son.

Your affectionate father until death,
Gray Jordan

William's younger brother Simeon did indeed join the war in 1862, and he fought with the 33rd Mississippi Infantry, Company C, in Mississippi, Georgia and Tennessee, along with his cousins Reuben, Crawford Newton, and Zachariah and many other residents of Lawrence County. For part of Simeon's time of service, he was the drummer for the company, and he was sometimes a litter bearer.[8] Although not in good condition at the time of Gray Jordan's letter, Simeon and most of the other Jordans in the 33rd were fortunate enough to survive the war[9] and live out long lives in the Brookhaven, Mississippi, area. William's younger brother James was out of the war by 1862, but he had returned to his wife and children permanently disabled in some way. His military record is confused and indicates that he went back into the war towards the end, but the records could have been about different soldiers. James's son, Samuel, joined the army later on in the war and lost an arm in battle.[10]

Gray's letter reflects not only the uncertainties of wartime existence in general but the effects of the war on the Jordan family. Certain family members were dead, others would never be the same, and hard times had hit with a vengeance. All the prosperity of the 1850s in Brookhaven had disappeared. Only older men and women were left to manage plantations and the few almost empty businesses. Union raids created a constant threat after the fall of New Orleans, the local college was turned into a field hospital and temporary cemetery, and a training facility for Confederate soldiers was constructed at Brookhaven because of the availability of the railroad. The training facility and railroad made Brookhaven even more of a target for raids by the union troops.[11]

Simeon Jordan

In Louisiana, the first real blow of the Civil War for the William Jordan family had been struck. Wyatt Jordan was gone. William had lost a beloved brother and become even more responsible for his brother's family. His frustration and rage combined to make his grief even worse. The war was becoming frighteningly real, and concern for the remaining boys in Virginia grew. The family could only wait and pray, hoping their boys would make it home but fearing the worst. However, they had yet to fully comprehend that the horrors of the war were only just beginning.

Camp, Bragg, Va May the 9 1863

Dear Sister I take my pen in
hand to drop you a few lines
to let you know that I am
well at this time pleded on gorge
is well they is a right smart
of sickness in camp anfen
nicett is sent to the horsepittle
he has the mompts times is very
late but the peple is just fixing to
plant corn the trees are just
begoine to put out their blooms
H O Bates is sent to the horsepite
and He Bates tell Jeff gives that
I send my love an best respes to
them I have not drone any thing yet
I sent my cloths of when we a
started on a march and I han d
not heard from them yet and I
dont much espee to
tell Eiza both he to tell the folk
howdy for me tell grenville
whiteone an an is to right to me
tell me that when I rite my

onely type to her by writing
g may gorge did not

send his I want you to
right to me I hav not heard
from home yet they have not ben but
one letter got in this company
yet Riley upsham got one
it was sent by hand to him
I heard that Sam chosnut was
dead & he then the meadoles and
was sent to the hospittle I have
nothing on importance you most
excuse my short letter I most
come to a close I hope these few
lines may find you all well
So I remain your affectian
Brother untile Death this to

Margarret J Jordan

J M Jordan

Peny I want you to take good
care of Scalam and make him
grow fast and I will
Pay you when i get back
and you must not pick him

The 27 86

Lawrence Co Miss July

Dear con I seat
my self to lop you a few lines to
you no that my family is not
very well at this time but is on
the mend we had the fever but on
the med at this time I was glad to
hear frome you all once more in
life I was sorry to hear that new
a bout your brother I want you to
write to me not in your
next letter dear son you said that you
had writen to me and hadent had no
answer but I had writen to you sence
I had a answer I thot the maile was
all dun away with your brother sim
is in the army I heard from hime
a few days ago is not very well at the
time your brother James is got a finel
discharge frome he a criple dear con
I can say that prospect for crops is
tolabe bad for we havent had raine
I think that if we get rain in a few
days that we will make genught
to make out on every thing is
high and scarce her salt especly
I think if eny hath will omit
I will com nex this faul to see you
all and get some salt dear son

I think that our countroy is in bad
fixs I dont no what will become of the
widows and children that is left
a lone her for all the men is gone
dear con your sister an family
is not well and is not bine well
all the sumer she a widow Mr hicmor
is dead dear son I harent eny thing
to interest you I want you to write me
when you get this dear son I must
sy somthing a bot my litle ochilden
I have three the smartes that you
ever saw two sons and one daughter
I must close my letter give my
love to all of my freindes and except
a dew portion for your selft
                      good by dear con
        your affection father
                      un til death
                      gray gorden

Chapter 6

No battlefield letters survived from the Jordan boys to their family in Louisiana in the period from May to August 1862. However the military record of their company listed several engagements in which the company took part. Undoubtedly, any and all of the Jordans who were well enough to be in the fighting participated because their letters home after July 1862 began to mention wounded soldiers, not just sick ones. The engagements listed for the company were Front Royal, May 23, 1862; Middletown, May 24, 1862; First Winchester, May 25, 1862; Strasburg, June 1, 1862; Cross Keys, June 8, 1862; Port Republic, June 9, 1862; Cold Harbor (Gaines' Mill), June 27, 1862; and Malvern Hill, July 1, 1862.[1] These were the names of ordinary places, towns, rivers, mountains, crossroads, farms, and churches in Virginia, but during the war they became the names of battle engagements where large numbers of men died. In this way, the names themselves became one of the casualties of the war because forever afterward they would be associated with the Civil War's carnage.

Front Royal on May 23, 1862, was a Confederate victory over the Union garrison stationed there, and it forced the Union army into retreat across northern Virginia to Winchester.[2] Major General T.J. (Stonewall) Jackson was in command of the Confederate troops, and he then engaged the Union forces under General Banks in another battle at Winchester (First Winchester) on May 25, completely routing the Union army and sending it in retreat across the Potomac River. Jackson's Shenandoah Valley Campaign needed this pivotal battle.[3] Two weeks later Major General John C. Fremont's Union forces, in pursuit of Jackson, ran into Major General Richard Ewell's Confederate division at Cross Keys on June 8. Forced to retreat, Fremont held a position that rendered him helpless to support the forces of General Erastus Tyler at Port Republic the next day on June 9.[4] Although the Confederates suffered heavy losses, they forced Tyler to retreat and cede control of the upper and middle Shenandoah Valley to Jackson who in turn was now able to reinforce Robert E. Lee in his defense of Richmond.[5]

Around the first of July, Lee attacked the Union forces under McClellan in several locations around Richmond. This became known as the Seven Days' Battles, with Malvern Hill on July 1 being the sixth and last of the series of battles. Lee suffered heavy casualties and gained nothing; however McClellan retreated to Harrison's Landing on the James River, thus ending the Peninsula Campaign.[6] Through all of this early fighting in May and June of 1862, the 9th Louisiana regiment, of which the Jordans' Company H was a part, suffered only light casualties.[7] In the next phase of the war, Major General T. J. Jackson engaged Major General Pope's forces along the Rapidan River, beginning the Northern Virginia Campaign.[8] On July 26, the 2nd Louisiana Brigade was formed with the 1st, 2nd, 9th, 10th, and 15th Louisiana regiments and Coppens' Zouave Battalion.[9] By August, Company H of the 9th Louisiana Infantry was camped at Gordonsville, Virginia. Floyd found time to write.

Gordonsville, Virginia
August 1, 1862
Dear Father and Mother,

I take my pen in hand to let you know that we are all well and in camp. Monroe [James] came to camp yesterday. He is not right stout yet, but he looks better than he has since he taken the measles and is still mending. He is a very steady boy in camp, more so than he was at home. You need not be uneasy about his getting into mischief. Tell Henry Babers' father that I heard from Henry yesterday, and he was coming to camp today. James Adams and Jack Holman are dead. Four of our wounded boys came into camp yesterday.

I want you to write soon, so nothing more at present only I remain your affectionate son until death.

F.H. Jordan

[On the back of the above letter was this one from brother James.]

Dear Sister,

I take my pen in hand to let you know that I have got back to camp again, but I aint very well yet. I just received a letter from Perry yesterday and was glad to hear from you once more in life. And I received the private note that you sent to me. Perry wrote that you had fine crops there, and I was mighty glad to hear that. And I want him to take care of Sealom till I get back home, if God will please to let me go home to see him. So I must come to a close by saying

Remember me till death
J.M. Jordan to M.J. Jordan

James Monroe had contracted the measles like his brother before him and was mending slowly, much to his disgust. His resistance was low which was dangerous considering his living conditions. Getting well, and staying that way, seemed nearly impossible for the Jordan brothers. On the other hand, as Floyd noted in his letter, other changes were occurring in James besides health-related ones. When James had been living at home in Louisiana before the war, he was evidently full of life and not adverse to getting into mischief, unlike his older, more steady brother, Floyd. The war and the illness that came with it was changing James. Growing up fast and feeling a lot older than his seventeen years, he was becoming a dependable soldier. However, his main interests still concerned home, neighborhood friends, and his horse, evidence of his youthful priorities. Conditions at home were good at this time. Northern Louisiana had not yet become the battlefield that Virginia had, and people continued to plant and harvest crops to make a living as well as support the war cause. It would not be until much later in the war that the North would realize that the way to bring the war to a close was to disrupt and destroy the Southern armies' supplies and support from the civilian sector. However, certain items were scarce and expensive even early in the war, and trade could not flow normally as a result of the Southern states being under blockade. Mail delivery continued to be wildly unpredictable, although the following letter from Floyd does indicate an occasional letter was getting through.

Gordonsville, Virginia
August 6th, 1862
Dear Father and Mother,

It is with pleasure that I take my pen in hand to drop you a few lines in answer to your kind letter which I received a few days ago. It was dated June the 5th. We are all well at this time. Monroe [James] isn't right stout yet, but he is mending. I have nothing of importance to write at this time.

We are expecting to have a fight at this place before long. I don't know whether it will be a big one or not. There has been some talk of our coming back to Louisiana but I doubt it. We have a very healthy time in camp now. Our boys are coming in every day or two. The wounded boys has almost all of them come in. I heard from Andy Bishop the other day. They said he was fat as a bear, but his wound was not right well yet. We are taken out of the 8th Brigade and attached to the 2nd.

I want you to write to me every chance, for I want to hear from home every two or three days. I reckon you will all have to eat my part of the watermelons and peaches. Lizabeth [sister] wrote here to know if I was going to write to her. I think I have wrote to her as much as she has to me and more too, because I write to her when I write to any of the family, without it is to Margaret, and I write to her to find out something about the girls, but I don't find out much then. And I would find out a heap less from her, without she has quit sitting in the corner and smoking her pipe. I will expect you all to write to me, but I may get defeated.

Tell Mr. Babers that Henry and James Holman has got back in camp and are both well at this time. Tell the old man Babers that I saw Darling about a month ago. He was wounded in the arm. I want you to write all about the crops when you answer this letter. They will be made by that time, I reckon, for I don't think we will get to come soon and see them, but I don't know. It is reported that England has recognized our independence, but I don't put much confidence in it.

The boys say it looks like their chance is bad if they have to stay away much longer, when it comes to the old widowers marrying the young girls. I will tell you what I am doing today. I am standing guard. So nothing more at the present, only I remain

Your affectionate son until death

F.H. Jordan

To his father and mother at home in Louisiana

Floyd described the mood in camp as upbeat because wounded troops were returning to action and the level of sickness in camp was down. In particular, he mentioned several of the Brush Valley neighborhood boys who had been wounded but had returned to camp. This news was intended for their families as much as for Floyd's own. For the first time, he mentioned the possibility of England recognizing Southern independence and sending support. The possibility of this happening was very real, especially early in the war, but he was right to mistrust rumors about it having already happened because it did not happen in 1862. He was also right to mistrust the rumors that some members of his company would be sent home to Louisiana on leave. That did not happen either. It had been a year since he had left home, and leaves were highly unlikely unless he were severely wounded. Soldiers were needed very badly with the battle casualty counts being so high.

He continued to express the concern of every soldier, that life would pass him by at home while he was away fighting. All the marriageable girls would be snapped up by the widowed men left at home. All the watermelons and peaches would be eaten by someone else, and the crops would be planted and harvested without his help. The things he most enjoyed in life were continuing at home, but he was not there to participate. On the other hand, Floyd's letter revealed a commitment to what he was doing in the war, even if it was only guard duty. Somehow, his service mattered. He also did not like being prodded to write to his sister Elizabeth who was George Bates's wife and not the source he had chosen for finding out news of the neighborhood girls in Brush Valley. His usual source for this information was his sister Margaret Jane, but even she did not always report as much as he would like to know. He teased her about sitting around too much and not gathering information to send to him.

Mary Elizabeth "Lizzie" Jordan Bates

However, Floyd was entirely correct when he wrote that a battle was looming for his company. In late July, he was one of the 14,000 men led by Major General T.J. Jackson and A.P. Hill who occupied the rail junction at Gordonsville. On August 9, 1862, a battle ensued at Cedar Mountain between Jackson's troops and Major General Nathaniel Banks' Union forces. The Confederates won the battle, giving Lee the initiative in a new fighting arena, Northern Virginia.[10] Jackson returned to Manassas to engage Pope's army on August 28. This battle would be known as Second Manassas (or by some, Bull Run) in the annals of the Civil War. The fighting began around Brawner's Farm and continued through August 29 where heavy casualties were incurred on both sides. On August 30, Pope renewed his assault on Jackson's troops, not realizing that Jackson had been reinforced by Longstreet. Longstreet threw his entire force of 28,000 men into the counterattack in the largest, simultaneous mass assault of the war. The Union forces were crushed and driven back to Bull Run at Centerville in not quite as large a defeat as First Manassas but almost. When the 9th Louisiana regiment ran out of ammunition on August 30, the men in furious fighting threw rocks at the attacking enemy soldiers until new ammunition could be brought up. The 9th regiment suffered one hundred casualties in this battle, their heaviest losses of the war so far.[11] After the battle, the Confederate Army of Northern Virginia moved on to Maryland.[12] They were on a roll.

Chapter 7

During Lee's Northern Virginia Campaign when the Army of Northern Virginia began its trek north after Cedar Mountain, one of the Jordans remained behind. James Monroe came down with typhoid fever and was sent to General Hospital #2 at Lynchburg, Virginia.[1] This was a large hospital in a complex of many hospitals where large numbers of Confederate soldiers were being treated for wounds and illnesses by an extensive staff of doctors and surgeons.[2] Even though he was receiving good care, he was already weakened from his bout with the measles, and he simply did not have the resources to fight off the fever. His condition continued to slowly deteriorate, culminating finally in his death on August 23, 1862.[3] He was buried in the Confederate Section of the Old City Cemetery at Lynchburg, Virginia.[4] James Monroe was seventeen years old and had seen little fighting in the six months he was in the war. Like his uncle before him, he never had a chance to contribute to the war effort with his fighting ability, and any contributions he would have made to his country by living out his life were destroyed as well. His death occurred before the battle at Second Manassas, but Floyd did not find out about it until afterward when the army had moved on to Maryland. Heartsick but resigned, there was nothing he could do but write home. He was the lone Louisiana Jordan left in the war, a circumstance that harkened back to the way things were in 1861 when he enlisted. 1861 must have seemed like a thousand years ago to him as a terrible loneliness shrouded his usual good humor.

Frederick, Maryland
September 9th, 1862
Dear Sister,

I take my pen in hand to drop you a few lines, as I get to send it part of the way by hand. These few lines leave me well.

George [Bates, brother-in-law] is complaining of being broke down. A letter came to the Captain yesterday from the hospital at Lynchburg that said Monroe [James] was dead. He died the twenty-third day of August. He died with typhoid fever. He was as good a boy as ever we had in our company. It is to be hoped that he is at rest, for I believe he was a Christian. I don't want you all to take it hard if you can help it. I hope the time will soon roll around when we can return home.

I think that Maryland will secede in a short time. She is making up troops for us as fast as she can. They are coming in day and night by gangs. We find more accommodation here than any other place we have been. They bring in milk and bread by wagon loads and give it to the boys. We can go to their houses and eat, and they won't charge us a cent. It is the prettiest country I ever saw.

I have nothing more at present, only I remain your affectionate brother until death.

F.H. Jordan

It mattered little that the course of the war was going well for the South when William and Martha knew that two of their loved ones, a son and William's brother, were not coming home and their other son was still in danger of suffering the same fate. They were terrified for Floyd, and also worried about George Bates, Elizabeth's husband. Frustrated and saddened beyond bearing and helpless to do anything else, William had another grim letter to write to his father in Mississippi. Floyd still held out hope that he would get to come home, but the war was not going well for the Jordans, and his situation grew more ominous every day. Maryland proved to be a vacation, a break from the threat of death, for a small space of time.

Floyd's hopes for Maryland's secession depended upon the continued success of the Confederate armies, and at that moment in the course of the war, it seemed as though Lee could not lose and the Union generals could not martial their forces enough to win. Floyd's comment about beautiful Maryland stood in stark contrast to what was about to happen there. The Civil War was fought on some of the most beautiful land in America, land that fortunately survived and recovered in spite of what men chose to do with it. The scars were left behind, however, and with them, a prevailing sense of sadness in silent testament to the war's destruction. Visitors to the battlefields, years after the war, would look upon the beautiful land and still feel a sense of melancholy, a ghostly reminder of lives ended too soon. The whispering wind sweeping across the landscape would seem to be the sighs of thousands of men who met in these places only to die.

Lee's next target was the Union garrison at Harpers Ferry. He surrounded it from the heights overlooking the town, and the garrison of 12,400 men surrendered with minimal resistance. Lee, along with Jackson a little later, was already moving on to Sharpsburg, Maryland. A.P. Hill stayed behind at Harpers Ferry to parole the prisoners, and then his orders were to join Lee.[5] Lee's primary purpose in going into Maryland was to find provisions and new soldiers for his army and secondly to move the war closer to Washington, D.C. and Pennsylvania. He succeeded in the first as Floyd's letter of September 9 recounted. Maryland provided good food and lots of it for the Confederate armies and many fresh soldiers. Lee succeeded in his second purpose just enough to arouse the Union armies under McClellan to try to halt Lee's invasion of Maryland and push him back into Virginia.[6]

The two great armies met on September 17, 1862, at Sharpsburg along Antietam Creek in the battle which would forever after be known as Antietam. The 9th Louisiana regiment had crossed the Potomac at Shepherdstown and formed its battle line on the evening of the 16th.[7] On the 17th, Lee was heavily outnumbered but managed to survive attack after attack with tremendous losses on both sides. The armies fought back and forth thirteen times across a cornfield near Dunker Church, the bullets and artillery mowing down the corn like a giant reaping machine and the soldiers of both sides with it. Other fierce fighting took place across a road bordered by a long ditch, later named Bloody Lane, and a bridge that was taken and retaken by both sides, later named Burnside Bridge after the Union general who insisted upon capturing it at any cost. Just as it looked as if Lee might be crushed, A.P. Hill arrived from Harpers Ferry to help turn back the Union forces at the end of the day on September 17th. The next day on the 18[8][th], Lee, while still skirmishing, orderly withdrew across the Potomac[8] at Shepherdstown, marching first to Martinsburg on the 21rst and then to Bunker Hill around October 5.[9] The North under McClellan chose not to continue the fighting, and through lack of aggressive pursuit, missed another chance to remove their most dangerous opponent.[10]

However, Lee had not won the battle, and this caused the European powers that might have helped the South to reconsider. It also gave President Lincoln the impetus he needed to issue the Emancipation Proclamation a few weeks later. Furthermore, Maryland did not secede from the Union. The battle was a draw with a terrible cost to both sides. In a single day on September 17 at Antietam, over 23,000 men were missing, killed, or wounded. It was the bloodiest day of the war, and the names Bloody Lane, Burnside Bridge, and Dunker Church would forever entail memories of terrible carnage.[11] The 9th Louisiana regiment suffered eighty-two casualties.[12] However, this time, fortune was with the Jordan family, and both Floyd and George Bates survived the battle.

Camps Near Bunker Hill, Virginia
September 30th, 1862
Dear Father and Mother,

I take my pen in hand to let you know that I am well at this time, hoping these few lines may come safe to hand and find you all enjoying the same blessing. George is well at this time. There is no fighting going on here now. We had the hardest fight in Maryland on the 17th day of September that ever was fought, I reckon. They say the Yankees acknowledge the loss of 30,000. I was right there myself, but I have no idea how many was killed, but they lay in piles. There was a great many of our men too. I have been in several hard fights, but that was the tightest place I have ever been in yet. I went in with my company, and when we came out, there was three of us left, besides what was gone to carry off the wounded. That was me and Gus Coleman and Bob

Vance. Bob and Gus both got slightly wounded, but not enough to stop them from traveling.

I have wrote to you once since the fight and I told you who got wounded. This is the fourth letter I have wrote to you since I have received any answer, but it does not put me out of heart. I hope the time will be when I can enjoy an earthly home with you all again. The Lord has spared my life so far, and I hope that He will be with me through the war. I want you to write to me as soon as you can. I have wrote to you about Monroe [James] every time that I have wrote. He died at Lynchburg the 23rd day of August. So nothing more at present only I remain

Your affectionate son until death
F.H. Jordan

To: W.H. Jordan, Brush Valley, Bienville Parish, Louisiana
From: F.H. Jordan, 9th Regiment, Southern Virginia

When Floyd first wrote home at the beginning of the war, and he had to report that someone had died, he was fairly unemotional about it, but he did communicate the feeling that death was still something unusual and worth noting. Life had some meaning, especially the lives of people that were known to him and his family. In this letter, Floyd calmly states that the dead "lay in piles." He was numb to the tremendous loss of individual life, perhaps because this was the only way he could accept it and go on. He could not afford to be emotionally involved in the battles and still survive mentally. Even if he survived the war and was able to return to his family, he would never be the same again. A part of him was gone forever.

After Antietam, Lee and the Army of Northern Virginia moved back into Virginia to the Bunker Hill area where Floyd wrote his letter of September 30 and then marched steadily south during the autumn to arrive at Fredericksburg on December 11 for the next major engagement with Union forces. The fall of 1862 was evidently a quiet period in the war in Virginia with no major battles being fought. Both sides were undoubtedly seeking to regroup after Antietam. No letters from Floyd to his family in Louisiana survived to give any insight into what he was doing. On October 5, the 9th regiment transferred back to the 1st

Louisiana Brigade in an exchange for the 14th Louisiana Regiment and was thereafter always associated with that brigade.[12]

According to his military record Floyd was on active duty through October 1862 and then was sent to the hospital at Winchester, Virginia, in November. He was listed as sick, but the disease was not given.[13] Had he been wounded at Antietam? This could have been the case, but he did not indicate that he was wounded in his September 30 letter to his parents. He had survived many hospital visits before, but this time was apparently different. He was very ill and unable to effectively fight back against the illness. Rather than hardening him, all of his previous illnesses and battles had lowered his resistance to a dangerous level. His condition continued to deteriorate over several weeks time, and his military record states that he died at the hospital in December of 1862.[14] No burial place was listed for him in Winchester, but in the years that followed, no more communication from him or about him was found in family records or letters. The bright young man with the wry sense of humor and concern for his family had followed his brother and uncle. As some consolation, this Jordan got his chance to fight, but disease served as his downfall, as it had from the beginning of the war. His family's worst fears were now realized. They had lost them all. William and Martha Jordan had other children, even other male children, but they suffered an incalculable loss with the deaths of their eldest two boys and William's closest brother. Of the immediate family members in the war, only George Bates remained alive at the close of 1862.

The 9th Louisiana Infantry Regiment remained intact and fighting until the final surrender of the Confederate army at Appomattox, taking part in every major engagement in the Virginia theater. It had the highest death rate of all the Louisiana units in Virginia - 233 killed, 349 died of disease, and 4 died of accidents.[15] Although this brigade was in the thick of the fighting all through the war, more men died of disease than were killed in battle, partly due to the living conditions and partly due to the fact that the Louisiana boys were far from their home environment. In the final cost accounting of the Civil War in the state of Louisiana, one-fifth of the state's able-bodied male population was killed, and many more thousands were left permanently disabled.[16] As proof of this, of the men that Floyd had mentioned in his letters home, many had died, many had been sent home permanently disabled, and only a few survived in the army to the end of the war.[17] The Jordan family experience was unfortunately not unusual.

September 30. 1862.

Camps near bunker hill Va

Dear father and Mother

I take my pen in hand to
let you no that I am well
at this time hopeing those
few lines may come safe to
hand and ny find you all
enjoying the same blesing
gorge is well at this time
I have nothing of importance
to right at this time they is
there is no fighting going hear
now we had the harest
fight in mariland on the 17
day of September that ever
was faught I recon they
say the yankey icknolage
the loss of 30 thousand

I was right there my
self but I have no
idea how many was killd
but they lay in piles
they was a great many of our
men too I have been in several
hard fights but that was
the the keybidest place I
have ever been in yet
I never is with my comp
and when we come out they
was three of us left besides
what was gone to carry off
the wounded that was me
and gus & colured and
bob me and bob and gus
both got slitely wounded
but not enuff to stop
them from traveling I have
road to you once since the

fight and I told you
who got wounded this is
the forthe letter I have
roat to you sense I have
received any answer but it
does not foot me out of
hart I hope the time will
be when I can enjoy a
arthly home with you all
a gaine the lord has spared
my life so fare and I hope
that he will be with me
through the war I wont
you to right be soo as soon
as you came ... ...
I have nout to you a brother
... every time that
... that I have roat he
died at linchburg the
23 day of august

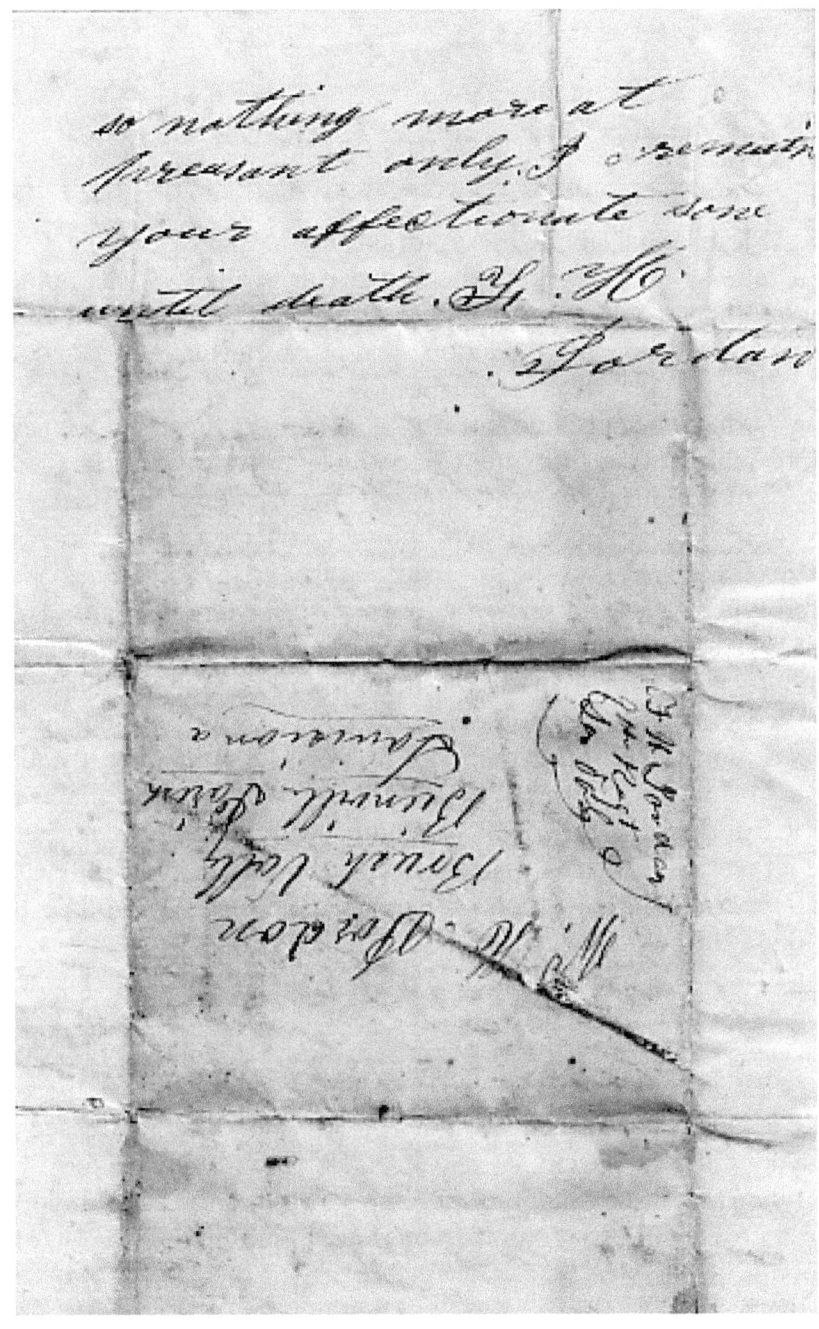

Chapter 8

"Mom, what about these Jordan boys who wrote the Civil War letters? Did they both die in the war or not?" I was hoping my mother would have some answers because she had been doing some work with the letters, and I was curious.

"The military records of the boys say they both died in the war," Mom began thoughtfully. "However, there are several things which cast a little doubt and create a mystery."

Now my curiosity was really up. "What things?" I asked.

"First, my mother always thought at least one of the boys survived the war, and she got that idea from her mother and other family members who knew the boys' sister, Margaret Jane. Why would this idea have persisted in the family if there was not some truth to it?" Mom paused for a minute. "Secondly, there is a marked grave site for James Monroe, but a grave site has never been found for Floyd, which is odd because he supposedly died in a hospital where he was identified and known. If he were buried in the same town where he died, why wouldn't they mark the grave if they had the information from the hospital? The marker could have disappeared over time, but why didn't the markers of the other soldiers buried in the cemetery disappear as well? This cemetery was apparently the only one where Confederate dead were buried in Winchester, so it is not likely that he would have been buried in another cemetery." Mom paused again. "And lastly, I found an envelope among the old letters in the trunk with no letter in it which was addressed to Floyd Jordan at Garvin, Texas. As far as I know now, there was no other Floyd H. Jordan in the family, but there was a Floyd G. Jordan, one of Perry Jordan's sons. Floyd's father, William, and Floyd's brothers lived at Garvin, Texas, in the 1890s. So, who knows?"

"Then, do you think Floyd died in the war or not?" I persisted.

"Until we can find some answers to my questions and some evidence to the contrary, we have to assume Floyd did die at the hospital in Winchester, Virginia, in December of 1862. But it's kind of nice, in the meantime, to think about the possibility that one of the boys survived the war and made it back to his family. Besides, I love a mystery, don't you?"

"Yeah. Mysteries are what got us into all this stuff in the first place," I sighed, knowing it would take a lot more years to find all the answers even if they could be found, and I was ready to get back to the juicy novel I had been reading before my curiosity got the better of me. After all, a high school kid could only live in the past for so long!

A final twist to the mystery occurred later. Mom always said there was another Civil War letter that disappeared from the collection after the collection had been loaned to a friend. If that letter contained a date that was past the December 1862 date of Floyd's death, then the mystery would grow even deeper.

Chapter 9

William Jordan had reached a breaking point. The home he had built for his family in Brush Valley, Louisiana, now felt like a prison with new disasters crashing down on him every day. He spent his days and nights going over the terrible truths that outlined the conditions of his life and that of his family. No matter how he analyzed his situation, his options were bleak and dangerous. By the late summer of 1863, the tides of war had turned. Vicksburg had fallen to the Yankees, and Gettysburg had been a devastating loss for Lee's Army of Northern Virginia. Up to this point, the fighting in Louisiana had been mostly in the southern part of the state, but it seemed only a matter of time until the armies would be coming to Bienville Parish.[1] William had lost two sons and a brother in the war, and he didn't want to lose the rest of his family.

"Martha, I tell ya I just don't like the way things are goin' with this war. It seems like things are all goin' the Yankees' way, and that means disaster here in Louisiana. Up to now, we've been lucky, but any time the Yankees could take a notion to come up here from New Orleans to our neighborhood. We're not safe anymore." William was reviewing his options again.

"I think it's too soon to say that," Martha answered back. "We need to give this some more thought."

"I've thought and thought," William rejoined, "and the risks of stayin' here keep growin' every day. And what's more, I can barely make a livin' in Louisiana anymore. We are survivin' and that's all. It's only goin' to get worse if and when the war ends, 'specially if the South loses."

"Well, what do you want to do? Go home to Mississippi?" Martha asked.

"Hell, no! It's worse in Mississippi than it is here, and I have little or no hope of gettin' any of Pa's land with his new wife and family makin' their claim on it. I would have to buy new land, so

why buy it where people are bein' attacked ever other day?"
William grumbled.

"Where would we go then?" Martha asked.

"I'm thinkin' our best chance is to the west in Texas where
land is plentiful and the fightin' is not as bad."

"But William, we don't know anything about that country
'cept people get scalped by the Injuns on a regular basis. I'd
rather take my chances with the Yankees, and ride out the storm
on familiar ground. Besides, all our friends are here and family
too with Wyatt's Martha and their kids," Martha argued.

"I know. This place has become home to us, and I don't want
to leave our friends either, but Martha, if the South loses the war,
our friends may be movin' too. Nothin' is goin' to be the same
here, ever again. As for Martha and Wyatt's kids, I am goin' to
try my best to convince them to come with us if we go. I hope I
can." William struggled with his doubts on this issue. As a final
argument, he put forth, "Remember when we moved here, we
were uncertain, but it worked out fine. If we have to go, it will
work out again."

"When we moved here, it took a lot of hard work to build
this place, and I don't look forward to doin' that again," Martha
got in the last word.

Discussions like the above took place on an almost daily
basis in 1863 until, after much soul searching, grief, and anger,
William finally decided to take his chances on the move farther
west to Texas. This, however, was not a popular plan with his
family who had grown to love their Louisiana home. William
was determined, though, once he had fought his way to a
decision, and Martha and the children were not going to refuse to
go with him, but they didn't like it. They were also going to lose
their close association with Wyatt Jordan's family because
Wyatt's widow, Martha, refused to leave her home in Louisiana.
William couldn't convince her to go. It was all she had left of
Wyatt besides the children, and she was not ready to give it up.
So it was with a great tearing wrench that in early September of
1863, William packed up his family and belongings, sold his land
to Isaac and William Frey, and headed west where hopefully life

had to be better.[2] He was taking a very big risk, but he felt he had no choice.

Within a few weeks of the sale of William's land in Louisiana, another family tragedy occurred. Gray Jordan died unexpectedly in Mississippi.[3] Whether William was notified before he left for Texas is not known, but it hardly mattered. He had already made his decision, and in his own mind, his father's death was the final blow that quite simply closed a door to his past. It would take years to settle his father's estate, years that he could spend building a new home and future in a new place. Whether he ever saw his remaining family in Mississippi again is not known. His life was taking a new direction.

As with many new endeavors, things were not better immediately. Traveling during wartime was hazardous at best, but the Jordans safely managed the almost-two-hundred-mile trip to the Palestine, Texas, area in Anderson County, in east-central Texas.[4] Leaving Louisiana when they did proved later to be a good plan because the Red River country of northwestern Louisiana that they traveled through to get to Texas would become a battlefield in 1864.[5] But they did not know this at the time they left their home, and so it was with continued uncertainty and sadness that they settled near Alder Branch, a small community close to Palestine, Texas, bounded by creeks and wooded areas. When William and his family drove their wagons into Alder Branch for the first time, they saw land similar to what they had left behind in Louisiana and Mississippi. The area was thick with pinewoods, and the creeks would sometimes turn into bogs with standing water. High humidity and insects abounded in the summer and fall months. However, scattered throughout the timber were areas of land that could be cultivated or used to raise livestock.[6] Anderson was one of the large cotton-producing counties in Texas that provided financial support for the Confederacy.[7] It was in this familiar-looking country that William decided to stay awhile and do some farming and ranching.

In the 1860s, often the first consequence of moving to a new area of the country was illness. The body would have to become immune to new germs in the new location, and the move itself caused extra stress on people, both emotional and physical, which would lower their resistance. The high humidity and insect infestation of the Alder Branch area also contributed to the Jordan family contracting fevers and other illnesses. Margaret Jane wrote her Aunt Martha in Louisiana about the family troubles and her lingering displeasure at having to move to Texas. Her aunt replied in the following letter.

State of Louisiana, Bienville Parish
November 26 [probably 1863]
Miss Margaret Jordan
Dear Niece,

I embrace the present opportunity of dropping you a few lines in answer of your welcome letter which came safe in hand and I was sorry to hear that you have had so much sickness since you have been to Texas. I was glad to hear that you had made plenty of corn to do you. Our corn was cut off short but I am in hopes that I have made plenty to do us the next year. The colery [cholera] has killed nearly all of our hogs and I don't know what we're to do for meat next year. It looks impossible to buy meat here but I hope there will be some money provided for us. We have some shoats that we can make meat of if the colery [cholera] don't get amongst them again.

Dear niece, I don't want you to think hard of me for not writing sooner for the mail is stopped and the letters can't pass. Tell Lizzie [Mary Elizabeth Jordan Bates, Margaret Jane's sister] that we heard from George [Bates] up to the 31rst of August. He was well and hardy. We heard that there has been fighting in Virginia. The news says that our side has been whipping them.

Dear niece, you said that you was coming to see us next summer. You don't know how glad I would be to see you. I would give more to see you all than anybody that I know of. The health of the people is tolerable good. There is a right smart bad cold about. Molly Pearce is sick. She has got the typhoid fever. She has been sick a good whole week. I will come to a close. I send my very best wishes to your family and receive a good portion for yourself so I must come to a close. Nothing more only I remain your affectionate aunt until death.

M.M. Jordan [Martha Jordan, Wyatt Jordan's widow]

Although William's family in Texas was sick and trying to adjust to a new place, conditions were worse in Louisiana. The economy was poor, as described by Martha Jordan to her niece, with no prospects of improvement. Martha and her family were all right and able to do some farming in the midst of war, but they had lost a large number of livestock due to disease. Martha was worried not only about money and income but also about the meat they would have to eat. People were also sick in her neighborhood. The only good news seemed to be that George Bates was still alive and apparently well in Virginia, at least at the last report.

Around Christmas time at the close of 1863, Margaret Jane received a letter from a friend who lived in her former home community in the Friendship area of Brush Valley in Bienville Parish, Louisiana. As was common for the times, it did not contain good news.

December 24, 1863
Miss Margaret Jordan
Dear Maggie,

With a broken heart I have to announce the death of my dear beloved one. My only hope on earth, my Absolom departed this life on the 8th of this month. Oh, Mag, I feel as if it will rush me to my grave, yet I hope you may never be so unfortunate as to experience it. It could not have hurt me any worse if it had been one of the family. But I hope that it is for the best. It is my loss but I trust it is his eternal gain. He written to me that he had a strong hope in heaven which is a great consolation to me. If he had lived, he would this day of been with me. They were on their march up to Monroe and Alexandria. He came in off of the day's picket and taken a congestive chill and he lived but three days. . . . . Colonel Walker sent his trunk home to Grandfather. I had the privilege of looking in his trunk and taking what I wanted. I taken his Testament and hymn book, his pens, paper, and envelopes, hair brush and comb and day book and neck tie and wafers and several other little things too tedious to mention. He had a few of my letters and that bouquet I gave him. He left here the 18th of last May for the last time. His pack and money did not come home yet. I wish you was here. I want you to come back. I am so lonely. I want some of my girl associates to stay with me. Margaret, if he had not died, what a different appearance all things would have had. Instead of mourning and weeping, it would have been the reverse. I mourn but not without a hope that I will someday be together with him to never part any more.

I am now writing on his paper and with his pen. I will write again when I hear how he died. I hope you will remember me in your prayers. I do not know whether I shall ever see you anymore, but let us strive to meet in heaven. Margaret, I have not heard from Henry [Babers] since you left [for Texas]. You know he was taken prisoner in August and is not exchanged yet. Mr. Bates got letters from George [Bates]. Tell Lizzie [Mary Elizabeth Jordan Bates] if she wants any of his letters, she must write to her father [father-in-law] and very affectionate too if she wants his letters which I know she does. From what I have heard he has very wrong opinions about Lizzie. He said he intended to pay for all of George's letters and take them. Father was down there. He saw a letter for Lizzie. I don't know how many was for her. One was written in October. James Holman was well. . . . . . .

Margaret, this is no Christmas to me at all. I have so many things to remember of him, so many letters and his picture. I am afraid it will never wear off. He said he wanted to be a married man. Write soon and often as I am done getting letters. My love to all.

Yours most affectionately,
Maddie J. Babers

. . . . . Mother sends her love to you and said she would of offered you a home when you was here [when the Jordans left for Texas] but was afraid it would hurt your mother's feelings and if you will come, she will give you a home. Give my regards to Lizzie. . . . .

Maddie Babers was obviously very young. She believed her life was over and she would not have any other relationships beyond the one she had lost. However, in spite of her inability to see the future in more optimistic terms, the pain of loneliness and separation she felt was genuine and felt by many during the Civil War. The Babers family, like Martha Jordan, were missing the Jordans and wishing they would return to Louisiana. Lost friends, lost relatives, lost prospective marriage partners. Lost was a good word to describe the condition of people in America, especially in the South, as a result of the war.

Maddie also revealed the unhappy relationship between George Bates' father and George's wife, Mary Elizabeth Jordan Bates. Mary Elizabeth had apparently decided to go with her family to Texas rather than remain behind in Louisiana to wait for her husband to return from the war. Whether this was the source of the ill feelings between George's father and Lizzie is not known. It could have been other matters as well, but in any case, Lizzie was going to have to petition her father-in-law in order to get her letters from George, and he did not seem in the mood to give them to her.

The year 1863 ground to a close with no end to the war in sight and not much cause for optimism in the South that the South would win it. The Northern armies were moving from the West on the Mississippi River to the Eastern seaboard and from the Northern states to the Gulf of Mexico, slowly squeezing out resistance as they went, but isolated areas still produced major battles. The war had taken a new direction with destruction and violence being directed towards the civilian population in the South in order to eliminate the Confederate armies' source of supply. Large battles between the Northern and Southern armies continued on unabated with high casualty counts, this being more significant for the Confederacy who had fewer men to lose.[8] Very few people in the South were looking forward to 1864 with anything but dread.

Chapter 10

The dawning of the new year in America, 1864, did not bring the optimism that a new year usually brings because the Civil War drug on and conditions in the South worsened with every passing day. The economy was undependable, the damage to land and property grew in the areas where fighting was taking place, and the death toll continued to climb. Wyatt Jordan's family was in the unenviable position of eye-witnessing the destruction of the South, most specifically of Louisiana. 1863 had seen extensive fighting in Louisiana along the Mississippi River, the sieges at Vicksburg and Port Hudson, and fighting at various locations in the southern part of the state. Conflict continued in 1864 in the southern and central part of the state, but it was mostly skirmishes and small battles.[1]

Martha and her children's letters to William's family in Texas described some of what was happening. Martha Jordan's oldest daughters, Caroline and Juliann, were approximately the same age as William and Martha's daughters, Margaret Jane and Mary Elizabeth. They had grown up together, so therefore, they quite naturally would try to write to each other, even though the mail delivery was slow and unreliable. Other friends and relatives also wrote to the Jordans in Texas about how their lives had changed. In answer the Jordans wrote about conditions in Texas where things were only slightly better because the economy in Texas was also depressed and some fighting was taking place. However, Texas was a big place with lots of room in which to move around, and in some areas, the citizens were too busy fighting Indians to worry about the Civil War. News from Louisiana was always eagerly anticipated, and the Louisiana Jordans felt the same way about news from Texas.

This January 1864
State of Louisiana
Parish of Bienville
Miss Margaret J. Jordan

Dear cousin,

It is through the kind mercies of almighty God that I have seated myself tonight to write you a few lines to inform you that we are all well and all on the land numbered among the living hoping when these few half written lines comes to hand that it will find you all in like capacity. Well cousin, I haven't anything very interesting to communicate to you. There has been several weddings and deaths since you left here. Miss Malica Collinsworth and Neuton Jones is married and Jack Worren and Cisire Gewin and Willson Bates and Mrs. Nancy Malone and I heard that Martha Williams was married but I don't know whether that is so or not and I don't know how many more. I will now tell you the deaths. Mrs. Ridle Hoover's baby and old man Fry, Norg Upshaw and old Mrs. Taylor I believe is all that has died since you moved off. The latest news we have from Virginia is the 4th of December. They have had another battle. The ninth regiment was sent off on picket guard and the Yankees came upon them and they drove them back with the loss of seven of our men taken prisoner. There is twelve missing out of Company H. George Bates, Jackson Fancher, two Dawkins boys, Asbery Crawford and David Brown. Don't know the names of the others. . . . Green was killed dead. That is about all the news I have.

Well cousin, I would have written to you before now but I have been waiting for a letter from you and began to believe I was not going to get one at all and I thought I would write you anyhow. I think you done me very bad. You have wrote to all the girls below here and I have never got the scrape of a pen from none of you yet. Ma got one from Elizabeth [Mary Elizabeth Bates] dated the 26th of October. I want you to write to me and write all about your new country and how you like to live there. Give my love and respects to all the family and receive a great portion for yourself. Tell Elizabeth that I will write to her before long and for her to write to me. Excuse my bad writing for my light is very bad. I must come to a close by asking an interest in your prayers to almighty God that if we meet no more on earth that we may meet in heaven where pain and parting is no more.

C. Jordan to M. Jordan

It was common among letter writers during the Civil War and afterwards to complain about not getting any letters. Their complaints were justified mostly because of the deplorable state of the mail where letters were often stolen or lost. Also, letter writers of this period had obviously been taught to begin and end their letters a certain way because the same conventional phrases appear in every letter. One of these conventions was to complain about not getting any mail. This particular letter from Caroline Jordan to her cousins in Texas contained some of these conventional phrases, but it also contained news concerning George Bates, Mary Elizabeth's husband, and it was not good news. He had been captured by the Yankees in a skirmish in Virginia. However, he was apparently not wounded or seriously injured, unlike some of the other men. The family would have to wait to see if he would be paroled by the Union forces and sent home. Mary Elizabeth, or Lizzie as she was known, was caught in a difficult situation. She was married, but she didn't have a husband. They had been apart longer than they had been together in their married life, and they had married young. Being a widow would have almost been easier to accept than the limbo in which she found herself. When her family left Louisiana, she chose to stay with them in Texas while waiting for her husband to return from the war because she could find some measure of comfort being with her family, and she apparently did not feel comfortable staying with her in-laws or by herself. Her husband, George, would just have to come find her in Texas when he got back from the war.

There was also news of the Brush Valley neighborhood and the marriages and deaths that had occurred since the Jordans had been gone. People were still getting married in the midst of war. Some were young people, but some were widows, created by the war, marrying older men in the neighborhood who had not become soldiers, a matter of survival for the woman in many cases. Even for single women still living at home, finding a husband was not an easy thing to do with most of the men gone. Some women married whatever man they could find just to have someone to support them. Oddly enough, the very thing that the young Jordan boys in the war had been worried about, that all the young women would be married by the time they returned home, was coming to pass. Before the Civil War, women in general had few options and were trained from an early age to think about marrying well. They usually did not work outside the home, and running a farm or business by themselves was not easy unless they had help with the hard labor. Taxes had to be paid from any income that they made, and the tax situation slowly worsened towards the end of the war and during the war's aftermath. Some women before the war were successful in business and careers usually thought to be held by men because they were capable, intelligent, and determined. This population of women grew during the war and afterward because there were often no men available to operate businesses and farms. Also, new careers for women in the medical field blossomed, signaling a change in society. However, most women still did not think to even try to be independent unless there was no other choice.[2]

In Caroline Jordan's letter, the reported deaths included the very old and the very young, a normal occurrence. No long lists of soldier deaths or flu epidemic victims were recorded. However, no one was taking life for granted. During this time, it could end for anyone with a lightning suddenness. Letters began and ended with references to life and death and meeting in the hereafter. Wyatt's widow used the same refrain in her letters.

Mr. W.H. Jordan and Mrs. M.J. Jordan
Dear brother and sister,

It is through the tender mercies of an ever merciful God that we are the special monuments of His amazing mercy while numbers of others have been taken from this world. I am thankful too that your most kind and welcomed letter came safe to hand and found us all enjoying a reasonable portion of health. We haven't had no serious sickness since you left here. The health of the people is tolerable good. I hope when this reaches you, that it will find you all enjoying the same blessing. You wrote to us how everything was selling. Everything is high enough and money is not worth much. Large bills in Confederate money don't pay at all. Tall corn has not been over five dollars yet. Cows is from $150 to $300 and I heard of one cow selling for $600. I don't hardly know what horses is selling for. Little ponies is selling for $500-$600. Bacon is two dollars per pound. I don't know what beef is worth. As for hogs, I don't know whether there is any for sale or not. Flour is from one dollar to one and a quarter a pound. I don't know what wheat is worth. Salt is two dollars per bushel. There is not as much business going on as there was when you was here, but they make a heap of salt yet. [Salt mines were close by at Winfield, Louisiana.] Cloth is not to be got at no price. Card [device for processing cotton] is $500 per pair from that to around six.

Crops is very injured in this settlement, but off farther around, they had rain enough and have very good crops. If I could see you, I could tell you a heap more than I can write. If you come back, I can't spare you more than one cow for I have lost three of my milk cows, and as for sheep, I don't know whether I can spare any or not. The soldiers killed some of them, the dogs or something else killed some of them, and they run with such a large flock, I can't count them, and I don't know how many I have got. I can't persuade you to come back nor to stay for I don't know what is best. That is about all I have to recite at this time. The girls have wrote all the news. We had a very pretty rain last night but not enough for a season. That is about all I have to write this time and I will close my short letter by asking an interest in your petitions to all mighty God that if we meet no more on earth that we may meet in heaven where pain and parting will be known no more.

Yours truly,
M.M. Jordan [Martha M. Jordan]

In every letter, the two Jordan families expressed their unhappiness at being apart. Used to being able to talk to each other about what was happening in their lives, they were now forced to write about these things. It wasn't the same. Some happenings they forgot to mention, and they had difficulty expressing opinions in writing. Conversation was so much easier. Martha in Louisiana had also not given up hope that William would come back and bring his family. She continued to offer encouragement in this area while leaving the decision to her brother-in-law. Even though times were hard, Louisiana was still home and the place to ride out the storm. However, with every passing day, the storm got a little worse.

Everything that had to be purchased, including animals and staples, was terribly expensive, and by 1864 Confederate money had lost its value and would not buy much. The war was not over, but already Confederate currency was becoming worthless, and the banks and lending institutions were in dire straits.[3] Fortunately the farms in Bienville Parish were largely self sufficient, but because of wartime conditions, things occurred to upset the normal self-sufficiency such as animals and crops being destroyed by troops. The Southern states were still under a blockade, so many things were unattainable such as cloth and ready-made clothing. The economy was so depressed that prices for crops and livestock were low even if the growing season produced anything to sell, and no one had any money to buy. On the other hand, animals of necessity such as milk cows, chickens, horses, and mules were very hard to find and very expensive. Transportation of goods outside of the South was impossible, and inside the South, transportation was disrupted by destroyed roads, bridges, and rail lines. Some businesses were still functioning, such as the salt mines at Winfield, Louisiana, but most business was depressed.

At this point Martha was managing to keep the farm going with the help of the children, but every day it got harder and more dangerous. Besides worrying about economics, she was constantly afraid that the fighting would eventually come to Bienville Parish. Until 1864, troop movements through the neighborhood had resulted in damage to crops and loss of livestock occasionally, but the serious fighting had stayed mostly in the southern and central part of the state. As long as Confederate resistance existed in the northern part of the state, however, the Northern armies would eventually feel that they had to eliminate it. The Union forces were also interested in controlling the Red River and capturing Shreveport. The rumblings had already begun about a Red River campaign led by General Banks being eminent.[4] It was only a matter of time, and time was running out.

this January the   1860
State of La   Parish of Bienville

                    Miss Margrit L forder
dear cozen it is through the kind mer
cies of all mighty god that I have seated
myself to knight to write you a
few lines to inform you tha we
are all well and all on the land
numbered among the living hoping
when these few half written lines
comes to hand that it will find
you all in like capacity well
cozen I havent any thing very
interesting to communicate to
you there has been several wedings
and deaths since you left here
Mary Malica collinsworth and
Newton jones is mariled and
Mr collinsworth and Mrs Cason
is mariled and old felon Coe and
Julia whitson is mariled and
Jac warren and Cazire gwin
and Willson Bates and Mrs
Nancy malone and I heard that
Martha williams was maried
but I dont whether that is so
or not and I dont know how
many more I will now tell
you the deaths Mrs Ridle hoovers
baby and old man frey Morgan
uppman and old Mrs taylor
I believe is all that has died since
you moved off the latest news
we have from va is the 1th of
dec they have had another
battle and the ninth reg
was sent of on picket gard
and the yankers came up on

them and they drove them

back with the loss of seven of
our men taken prisoners there
is thelve missing out of Co H
George Bates Jackson Rancher two
dawkins boys Asbery Crawford
and david brown I dont know
the names of the others _ Green
was killed dead that is about
all the nuse I have well soon
I would have written to before
now but I have been waiting
for a letter from you and be
gan believe I was not going to
get one atall and and I thought I would
write you any how I think you
dont me very bad you have
wrote to all the girls below here
and I have never got the scrape
of apen from none of you yet
you got one from Elizabeth
dated the 26 of oct I want you
to write to me and write all a
bout your new country and
how you like to live there give
my love and respect to all the
family and receive a great
portion for yourself Tell Eliz
abeth that I will write to her
sis ____ and let it
avale to me excuse my bad
writing for my light is very
bad ____ come to a close by ____
___ an interest in your prayers
to all mighty god that if we meet
nomore on earth that we may meet in
heaven where pain and parting is nomore

Chapter 11

In the spring of 1864 the William Jordan children in Texas were still not very happy with their new home, and they were missing their friends and relatives back in Louisiana. Although conditions were precarious in Louisiana, it still seemed wrong to be living in Texas, apart from the life and the people they had known for most of their lives in their former home. Their friends and family that they had left behind were missing them as well. At this time a letter arrived containing news of some of the men from Company H, 9th Louisiana Regiment who had been captured by the Yankees, but still there was nothing about George Bates. All of the captured soldiers were being released and some were coming home to Brush Valley in Bienville Parish on furlough. It was a long trip home to Louisiana from Virginia, and the men would have to find their own transportation. Wyatt's daughters were writing to their cousin Margaret Jane in Texas about this.

April the 23rd, 1864
Bienville Parish
State of Louisiana
Dear cousin Margaret,

I again seat myself to drop you a few lines in answer of yours the 28th of February, and I read it with pleasure and I was sorrowed to hear that you was so dissatisfied and that you could not get our letters. We have wrote I don't know how many letters. We have answered every letter that we have received from any of you, cousin Margaret. I have nothing of importance to write you. I wish you was here to go to church tomorrow with us. We are all well except Ma. She has got the neuralgia in her eye. Well, Hubberd Alexandra has got home. He got home last Sunday. They was all paroled to Richmond and there was some of them got furlows to go to Mississippi and Mr. Alexandra came home and they are looking for Jackson Fancher now and I have not heard whether George has got any furlow or not. Dear cousin, you don't know how bad I want to see you. If I could be with you one hour, I could tell you more than I could write in a week, dear cousin Margaret. The girls always they would be glad to see you all. I have received two letters from you and one from Lizzie. I answered them. The Yankees is down on the Red River. They have had several battles there, but our men has backed them out every time. Dear cousin Margaret, Nancy Raborn has been lying very low with the pneumonia but she is mending. Tell Aunt Martha that I have not forgotten her and hope she will remember me. Tell Lizzie I wrote her a letter last Sunday. I want you to write as soon as you get this letter. This is the third letter that I have wrote and you wrote to me that you have not received but one letter from me.

Dear cousin, I want you to write often. Well I must come to a close so nothing more only I remain your affectionate cousin until death.

Miss Juliann Jordan

Dear cousin Margaret,

I will drop you a few lines to let you know that I have not forgotten you and I hope you will remember me. You must excuse me for not writing however I want you to write as soon as you get these few lines. I wish I could see you. I am going to school now. I wish you was here to go to school with me. Well, I must come to a close so nothing more only I remain your affectionate cousin until death.

Miss Emily Jordan
Miss Tabitha Jordan

Martha's younger daughters were growing up and could write letters of their own now to their older cousins in Texas. Caroline and Juliann continued to send any news that they could remember to put in a letter, usually getting ahead of their mother, but letters were frustratingly slow and could not make up for the cousins not being together. Furthermore, the news of the neighborhood was not very cheerful as a rule.

Between the Jordans in Louisiana and the Jordans in Texas lay the Red River and Mansfield, Louisiana. The last major battle of the Civil War in Louisiana was fought there in early April of 1864 as a part of the Union forces' Red River campaign. The Union troops under General Nathaniel P. Banks marched north in force to take control of the northern half of Louisiana and planned to eventually launch an invasion of Texas. Southern troops massed south of Shreveport to counter the invasion force. On April the 8th, the Southern troops under General Richard Taylor's command met the first regiments of the Union army just south of Mansfield at Sabine Crossing and after a pitched battle, seized the momentum, forcing General Banks' troops into a disorganized retreat to Pleasant Hill.[1] Bank's cavalry and one division of infantry had been in the thick of the battle outside of Mansfield, but when they began to retreat to the south, they had no choice but to take to the woods because the only road available was narrow and clogged with supply trains which had been moved too far to the front and then not been removed in time. Reinforcements were also having a hard time getting past the supply train to the front lines of the fighting arena. In addition, the road was in miserable condition because of the early spring rains.

The fierce fighting raged for miles outside of Mansfield,

through the woods where confusion reigned, and all the way to Pleasant Hill, causing a huge number of casualties. The Northern army's supply train, trapped on the road, was abandoned, and many artillery pieces were lost to the Confederates as well as the supplies. Banks had made two tactical errors. He separated his land forces from his naval forces by using the stage road approach to Shreveport (The navy on the Red River was too far away to help him and was busy fighting for its own survival), and he separated his advance troops from reinforcements with his supply trains.[2] On the second day, April 9, the fighting commenced in front of the town of Pleasant Hill and continued all day, completely destroying the town and increasing the casualty count to even higher numbers.

Pleasant Hill Battlefield Memorial

Again, it was ironic that a place named Pleasant Hill should be the scene of such bloody fighting. A sign marking the battlefield at Pleasant Hill reads, "A terrible sight met the eyes of those who braved the field of carnage on that Sunday morning. Many thousands of dead, dying, and wounded men lying as far as the eyes could see were intermixed with well over a thousand dead horses and broken and scattered equipment." The Union armies left in the night and retreated to Natchitoches, Grand

Ecore, and further south, leaving the dead and wounded where they fell. The dead were buried in a mass grave on the site of the destroyed town by the returning townspeople the next day, and the town of Pleasant Hill was rebuilt after the war in a new location.[3] Unfortunately, the battle which had cost so many lives was indecisive, but Banks retreated to New Orleans anyway with the Confederate army nipping at his heels and skirmishing for as far south as they dared, thus delaying the end of the war in Louisiana and Union victory by several months.[4] Pleasant Hill was the last major battle of the Civil War fought in Louisiana, and it ended the Yankee's Red River Campaign.[5] The claim has been made that this was the largest battle fought west of the Mississippi during the Civil War.[6]

With the arrival of the Louisiana Jordans' April letters, concern grew in Texas for the safety of the family left behind. What William Jordan had been afraid would happen was coming to pass. The fighting was now close to Bienville Parish, only about sixty miles away at the Red River. Wyatt's widow, Martha, wrote some of what was happening but refused to let the war consume her entire letter.

24th of April 1864
Mr. W.H. Jordan and some to all the rest
Dear brother and sister and nieces,

I seat myself this evening to inform you that I have not forgotten you yet and I hope you still remember me. We are all well except my eye. I have got the neuralgy in it and am not doing very well. The Yankees have not been here yet but I don't know how soon they may come, but I hope they won't come at all. They are fighting every two or three days on Red River. They have burned up country and destroyed several things. The Negroes are going to the Yankees every day. I have not news from Virginia except that all the prisoners that was taken in Richmond when George was is paroled and Hubbard Alexandra has come home and we are looking for Jackson Fancher every day. Well, I will drop that subject.

There has been a great deal of cold weather this winter and spring. Crops look very small and bad. I am sending my children to school; the boys is plowing out my corn now. Wheat crops look pretty unless the drought cuts it off. It is very dry, cold, and windy but it looks like rain today and I hope it will rain before many days.

Well, Martha, I would like very much to see you, but as the distance is so great that I can't see you, I want you to write to me for I have never received a word from you yet. I want you to write to me how you are doing, and I have wrote several letters to you all and received but a few. Tell Liza that I haven't forgot her yet. I have wrote to her a few times. Well, Margaret I will send you a few words so that you may know that I haven't forgotten you. I am sorrowed to hear that you was so dissatisfied. If I could help you any, I would willingly do so. You wrote to me to send you the Lay Baptist, but I can't send it for they haven't got the paper to print on. I want you to write to me often. The children all sends their love and respect to you all. I want you all to write us all as often as you can and I must write a few to Liza about George. Mr. Crawford was here a few minutes ago. He saw Alexandra and talked with him. He said that George was paroled and come with him to South Carolina and said he was well and hardy and did not have a crutch or a boil on him. He said he expected that George was on his way to our place. I will come to a close so nothing more only I remain your sister until death.

M.M. Jordan

At last there was some good news concerning George Bates; he was apparently all right and on his way home. However, he had a long and perilous journey ahead of him in order to get home to Louisiana and then on to rejoin his wife in Texas. He was most likely traveling by foot and catching rides on wagons when possible, trying to avoid enemy troops and becoming a prisoner again. The Jordans would have to wait to see if he would make it back in one piece.

Even in the midst of war, everyday life went on. Children went to school, the crops were planted and harvested, and the weather took its toll. However, there was no paper on which to print the church newspaper, so this part of everyday life was different. Margaret Jane would have to get her news of the church family from letters. Getting this news from her aunt would certainly not lighten her spirit much.

Although the last of the large battles in Louisiana during the Civil War had taken place in early April at Mansfield/Pleasant Hill, small skirmishes were still being fought all over the state. As Martha reported in her letter, the fighting was getting very close, and soldiers from both armies tromped through the neighborhood, taking what they needed. Then, as if the constant threat of having a battle break out in their own backyard, low income from their crops, and not enough to eat were not enough to worry about, in June of 1864 a flu epidemic swept through the Brush Valley community. During this savage Civil War time period, death came in many ways, and it must have seemed at times as if life did not stand a chance against it, but the people, especially the young, found ways to survive and even thrive. Wyatt's daughter, Caroline, then nineteen, wrote to her cousin Margaret about the flu epidemic, as well as the progress of the war.

June the 5th, 1864
Miss Margaret J. Jordan
Beloved and affectionate cousin,

It is through the kind providence of Almighty God that I embrace the present opportunity of dropping you a few lines in answer to yours of the 18th of March which came safe to hand after so long a time and found us all well, and I hope that when these few badly written lines come to hand, they will find you all well and hardy and doing well. The health of the people is tolerable good. There has been a good deal of pneumonia this spring but none of us have had it yet, and I hope we won't have it at all. The flux is raging now. Henry Raborn's family is all down with the flux now. Betsy Harris' baby died week before last, and old man Woolly lost three of his family, his wife and his two single daughters. They are dying up around Sparta with it. I heard the other day that Mrs. Blackwood had the flux, but I don't know whether it is or not.

Becky Taylor's baby is dead. A soldier died at Johnson Fancher's about two weeks ago with the typhoid and pneumonia and consumption all together. Old Mrs. Laird is dead. I believe that is all I haven't wrote about. Well cousin, I hardly know what to write. Crops look very well considering the cold weather we have had and drought too but we had a very pretty rain the other day. Well cousin, I hardly know what to write. I haven't got any late news from Virginia. I have wrote you all the news before.

John T. is at home yet. Columbus Raborn, Thomas Blackwood, Faris Whitlock, Rals Loe has all went to the army and H.P. Collinsworth is riding the courier line. None of the Virginia soldiers hasn't went back, but some of them has joined the army here in the South. Well, Margaret, you ought to have been here about two weeks ago to see the soldiers. There was three divisions - Walker's, Scurie's, and Churchill's. Some of them was nice looking men. Churchill's division camped along Pine Ridge two nights and one day. We all went to see them and hear the music and see their artillery. You wrote to know who was killed. No, there was not nobody killed that I was acquainted with. There was several officers killed. You wrote that we did not write often enough but you know how often we wrote. My pen was so bad that I quit writing with it and taken my pencil. Excuse my bad writing and spelling and all mistakes. Give my love to all the rest of the family and claim a double portion for yourself.

Your cousin,
C.E. Jordan

Dear cousin, I would give more to see you than anybody else on top side of this earth. Then I could tell you what I want to and could ask you a heap.

The flux epidemic caused many deaths in the area, and this letter also reported the death of a soldier. This was an unusual occurrence for the neighborhood because not much fighting took place there, and sure enough, this soldier died of disease rather than battle wounds. Fortunately the Jordans managed to avoid the epidemic this time. They seemed to remain healthy which was a blessing considering all the other hardships they had to endure.

This letter revealed one of the occasions during the war when community members could celebrate the war rather than curse it. Reviewing the troops created great excitement and enthusiasm among a war-weary populace, especially for a young woman just coming into her own. The music, the artillery, and the men in uniform must have seemed exciting to the people in the neighborhood, even though the Confederate army was in pretty sad condition by 1864. The war had lost its romance and glorious arrogance, but small stirrings of excitement and patriotic fervor still remained.

What a time to grow up! In normal times Caroline and Margaret Jordan, their sisters, and friends would have been concerned primarily with going to social events, meeting the right men, and eventually getting married. However, because of the war, young women were not even sure if there would be any men left alive to court and marry them. In their letters, they wrote about who was killed in the fighting rather than who attended the latest party, and there were no men around to escort them to parties anyway. Even in 1864 the men who came home for a short while from the war returned to their units or joined units closer to home. William Jordan's younger daughters would not be marrying Louisiana men as they had once thought, and only William and Wyatt Jordan's oldest daughters married in Louisiana. Their lives were forever changed and turned in new directions by the war. Change became the norm rather than the unusual, and young people had to learn to adjust. Adjust they did, in many ways better than their parents, helping to create a new society for their children and grandchildren.

April the 23 1864

State of La Bienville Parish

Dear cousin margret
I again seat my self to drop you a
few lines in answer of yours the 28 of
_____ and I _____ it with pleasure
and I was sorrow to hear that was
so ill satisfied and that you could not
get our letters we have wrote I dont
know how many letters we have _____
every letter that we have received from
any of you cousin margret I have nothing
of importance to write you I wish
_____ _____ _____ _____ _____ _____
mamaw is till us we are all well except
ma she has got the new _____ in her eyes
well hubberd alexanra has got home
he got home last monday they was
all paroled to ritebuond and there
was some of them got furlows to
go to mississippi and _____ alexanra
home and they are looking for
_____ _____ _____ _____ I hav not
_____ _____ _____ george has got any
furlow or not _____ your aunt
_____ _____ had I would to see you
if I could describe you one _____
I _____ _____ _____ more than I
could write in _____ dear cozen
margret the girls _____ they
_____ _____ _____ you at I
have _____ two letters from you
and one from lizza Hanerird thu
the armey is down _____ _____ they
have had several battles there but
our men has backed them out very
fast dear cozen margret nancey
_____ has been lying very _____

with the memory that she is
missing tel aunt martha that I
have not forgotten her and hope
she will remember me tel her I
wrote her a letter last month
I want you to write as soon as you
get this letter this is the third letter
that I have wrote and you
wrote to me that you haven't recei
ved but one letter from me
dear cousin I want you to write
often and I must come to a
close as nothing more only I
remain yours affectionate cousin
until death

        Miss marget gordan
          Miss julean gordan
dear cousin martha I will drop you
a few lines to let you know
that I have not forgotten you
and I hope you will remember
me you must excuse me for a
written nearly I want you to
write as soon as you get these
few lines I wish I could see you
I am going to school two days a week
you was here to go to school with
me and I must come close
to at about something to
only I remain your affectionate
cousin until death

        Miss Emali gorda
        Miss tabitha Markeun

Chapter 12

July 1864
Pine Ridge, Winn Parish
Louisiana
Dear Mag,

After awaiting a long time, I once more attempt to communicate you a few lines to let you hear from me once more. I received your kind letter two weeks ago but was rather dilatory in responding for which I beg your forgiveness. It was not for want of affection that I did not write any sooner but a little neglect - well, I will try and tell you my reasons. When I received your letter, I taken the toothache and a pain in my head and face. I had my tooth drawed, but I still have a pain in my face and when any set time came to write, I went to Saline meeting. I enjoyed myself finely. There was nine joined the church. I saw them baptized. A preacher from Walker's Division came on a week's meeting there. He is a great preacher. Jane Austen and two other young ladies joined, Mr. Sprawls' son and Prothro's son and four Negro boys and also Miss Marrita Sprawls was restored.

Well Mag, I have some good news to tell you as well as bad. I received a packet full of letters yesterday, one from Cousin J.A.W. and some from S.C. They were old but we were happy to get them. Cousin James' letter was dated April 2. He was well and hearty. He said he had heard from Henry some time ago. He was well and in fine spirits. All that report on him was false. Mag, a great many people has died since you left here with flux. Mr. Welby's wife and two daughters and son died in less than three weeks. Old Mr. Henry Rabon and wife. Grandfather is very sick. He has been in bed a week. Dr. Owen tended him. They have give him up and I think he will take his leave in a few days. We hate very much to give him up, but I reckon we will.

Dear Mag, I am plaiting and making hats every day. I have

made $70.00 and if nothing happens, I will collect $25 next week. I plaited Catherine a hat - a very fine plait. It is a beautiful hat trimmed with roses and a different shape to what any hat was. I am going to plait me another. Mine is too coarse and ugly. A great many has spoke to me to make them hats. I would not work for this money if it was not for paying taxes. Our taxes will be near 600 dollars and we cannot pay it unless I can make it. Father has been home four weeks but will leave in a few days. He is very unable to go. Catherine has been right sick for three days with fever. I saw Melissa and Dora last Sunday at church. Martha Williams remains single yet - I don't know of any readings in a long time. I heard Gus Lord was killed. His mother is dead. Rip Shaw's son's leg is taken off. He is gone after him. We heard Henry was in South Carolina, but I reckon he is not.

Mag, this is for you and Eliza both, and you must excuse my hand writing, and I will try and do better next time. I will tell you I am going to do my part yet and write a pretty letter before long and send across the river. I am going to have it well needleworked. I wish you were here to eat watermelons with me and drink wine and eat cake with me. I made a gallon of blackberry wine. I am going to make grape wine if I can get enough grapes. Mag, I wish I was there with you across the river or I wish you were here. I am tired of this neighborhood. It seems like Carolina church will go to nothing and when I leave here, that is all that I will have to leave behind is our church beliefs. I have written everything I can. Write to me.

To M.J.J.   E.B. Lee and J.B. Lee

This letter to Margaret Jane Jordan in Texas from her friend in Louisiana is the last of the surviving letters written from Louisiana to the Texas Jordans in the closing days of the Civil War. It bore some news of friends and family, but it also reflected the general feeling of depression among community members over the state of the war and of conditions in Louisiana. People were sick and dying because of the flu epidemic. Women were finding it difficult to marry and find security in the same way they had always found it in the past. Taxes were high, and people were working in odd new ways to make enough money to pay them. Often families had to persevere without the head of the household to provide an income because he was dead or away with the war. Entire estates could be lost to the tax collector, so landowners and their families felt they had no choice but to do whatever was necessary to keep their land. This situation would not improve with the end of the war. A great number of land parcels changed hands during this time due to the death of the owner or his failure to pay the taxes on the land. The courts were clotted with cases of probate settlement and guardians being appointed for children who had lost their parents.[1] Friends and relatives were separated, sometimes permanently. Those men who returned from the war were often disabled, their health impaired permanently.[2] The old way of life in Bienville Parish was dying, and people were struggling just to survive and not die with it. However, one positive note in the midst of these depressing conditions proved to be that people through their struggles found a new strength and creativity. They did things that only a few years earlier would have seemed impossible. As related in her letter of 1864, Mrs. Lee was making hats.

In the last months of 1864 and the early months of 1865, the Civil War continued, but soldier morale was low, and when Robert E. Lee surrendered his armies in Virginia in 1865, it was the beginning of the end. More surrenders of Southern troops occurred, and the men also began to desert and go home. Slowly, in every state in the Confederacy, final resolutions were made to end the war.[3] In Louisiana, although the war was over and the fighting ended, the economy was destroyed, the former slaves were citizens, and many people were either dead or had moved away. Louisiana had emerged from the war with less than half its former wealth, less than half its livestock, and its land stripped and bare.[4] It was not the same world as before the war, and the question became for the Jordan family, how long would Martha Jordan continue to struggle with the situation in Louisiana, knowing that conditions could not improve for a long time.

During this time the Jordans received bad news concerning George Bates; he did not return from the war to Louisiana. In spite of reports to the contrary, George was not well and unharmed. Apparently after being captured by the Yankees and paroled in 1863, he was captured again and paroled once more. He went to the hospital in late 1864 where he was captured again and thereafter was transferred from hospital to hospital until he eventually died at the close of the war in 1865.[5] Mary Elizabeth (Lizzie) Jordan Bates was left a widow in Texas before she ever had a chance to be a wife. Sadly, the William and Wyatt Jordan families had lost every family member that had gone to fight in the Civil War, and none of them had died in battle. They all died of disease. The Jordans were unfortunately an example of many Louisiana families that paid a disproportionately high price in the war.[6]

In Texas, the economy was not good, but conditions were slightly better than in Louisiana. No destruction due to fighting had taken place in the Alder Branch area or anywhere near it. Most of the hardships people had to bear were caused by the economy, crop failures, and epidemics or illness. William and Martha were farming and raising livestock and had begun to interact with the community at Alder Branch, in particular with three other families who had settled near Alder Branch in the 1840s and 50s. These families were the Fergusons, Huddlestons, and Squyres. The Mortons and Killians were also prominent families in the neighborhood and were related to the Fergusons, Huddlestons, and Squyres by marriage. When families in 18th century America emigrated to new areas, they often traveled in large groups of relatives and friends, ensuring safety and a ready-made neighborhood when the group arrived at the new location. This had been the case with the Fergusons, Huddlestons, Mortons, and Killians. They formed a tight-knit community in the Alder Branch area.[7] In the early years in Texas, they often had encounters with Indians, mostly nonviolent but not always. As new emigrants to Texas, they tried to locate themselves close to military forts for protection, but as the years passed and the situation eased, they moved out to settle the countryside.

William "King" David Ferguson was born around 1802 in Lancaster Co., South Carolina, the son of John and Nancy Ferguson. He emigrated to Blount County, Alabama, and married Mary Elizabeth Morton, the daughter of John M. and Nancy Morton on December 28, 1825. William Newton Huddleston was born around 1808 probably in South Carolina and emigrated to

Blount County, Alabama, where he lived close to William Ferguson. He married Jane Morton, another daughter of John M. and Nancy Morton. In 1837, the Huddlestons and the Fergusons moved to Texas along with their neighbors, the Goodwin Killions. The Mortons came along as well. They lived first near Fort Duty, but they moved to other locations because of the Indian trouble and finally settled in the Alder Branch area on Snake Creek.[8]

"King" David Ferguson and his wife Mary had eleven children, five boys and six girls. Four of the five boys fought as cavalrymen in the Civil War in Texas and returned home after it ended to become farmers and ranchers. One also became a minister. His name was John Thomas, and his brothers were Hughlet Newton, William David, Jesse Jasper and David. Their sisters were Dicey Jane, Nancy, Elizabeth, Amanda, Mary, and Caroline Delilah.[9] William Newton Huddleston and his wife Jane had eight children, seven boys and one girl. At least three of the boys fought in the Civil War in Texas and all were farmers and ranchers after the war. They were John Patrick, William E., Lewis P, James A., Daniel C., Joseph N., Rusk, and Martha was the lone girl. The Huddleston children and Ferguson children were cousins as their mothers were sisters. Some of these children married Killions, and some married into the Squyres family.[10]

The John W. Squyres, Sr. family was one of five separate Squyres families, originally from South Carolina and then Louisiana who moved on to Texas. They were all related, with John W. being an uncle to three of the heads of household and a father to the other one. John W. Squyres, Sr. was a Hardshell Baptist minister who fathered eighteen children by two wives. Seven of his sons and one grandson fought in the Civil War. He farmed on land near Alder Branch Creek.[11]

William H. Jordan and his family quickly recognized the Alder Branch community's organization into family groups, and they felt right at home with this situation because they originally came from a similar tight-knit community in Mississippi. When William arrived at Alder Branch in 1863, the most valuable possessions he brought with him to the new community were his daughters. After he had lived there for a few years, his girls

caught the attention of the unmarried male population in Alder
Branch, recently returned home from the Civil War. Although
one of his daughters, Margaret Jane, had been unhappy to be
living in Texas for these years, by the end of the war in 1865, she
had met and married John Thomas Ferguson, the young minister

John Thomas Ferguson in Later Years

and farmer son of William "King" David Ferguson. Alder Branch
truly became her home and would continue to be her home, off
and on, for the rest of her life. She and John were married on
October 12, 1865.[12]

    Scarcely three months later, her sister, Mary Elizabeth
(Lizzie), widow of George Bates, married Harmon Van Squyres
on January 8, 1866.[13] Harmon was one of the seven sons of John
W. Squyres who fought in the Civil War in Texas. He served
mostly along the Rio Grande, and he also took part in the last
battle of the Civil War at Brownsville, Texas.[14] After the war he
was a farmer and carpenter. Mary Elizabeth had not remained a
widow for long, but this was common practice for women in the
uncertain times during and after the Civil War. Even when
remarriage was not a matter of survival as in Lizzie's case, all the
former conventions of lengthy mourning seemed to be cast aside

by the people of the post war period. These conventions simply didn't hold much meaning anymore with death so prevalent. Life and living were what mattered because no one knew how long his or her life would last.

On the 14th of August, 1866, Margaret Jane and John Ferguson's first child was born at Alder Branch, a son named David. Lizzie and Harmon had their first child a year later in November of 1867, a son named William Fletcher.[15] Grandparents William and Martha Jordan enjoyed watching their family grow once more instead of shrink, and concentrating on new life was certainly better than dealing with death. They were healing and finding some peace, learning to accept the sadness that the war had brought and to look with some optimism to the future in a vast new land.

However, in spite of the arrival of his first grandchildren, by 1867 William had become restless and impatient with his current circumstances. He was ready to move on to a better place. He had heard of good land in Henderson County, healthier country, so he packed up his family and followed the road north to some land outside of Athens, Texas, but he was actually only moving about fifty miles from Alder Branch. His daughter Margaret Jane and her family moved as well, but Lizzie and her family decided to remain at Alder Branch, close to Harmon's parents and siblings.[16] By now, William Jordan's wife, Martha, had given up and was resigned to moving every few years, and her sons, Perry and William, probably thought it was a great adventure to be on the move. Her daughter Martha was perhaps the only one in the family who was not very happy about moving because she had made friends among the young people at Alder Branch, in particular a young man named Daniel Huddleston, a cousin of her sister's husband, John. Daniel was the son of William Newton Huddleston, head of one of the interrelated families living at Alder Branch which had already claimed two of William Jordan's daughters. In any case, 1867 found the William Jordans in a new home in Henderson County, Texas, while one of their daughters, Mary Elizabeth, was starting her own family life in Anderson County.

The Jordan Family in Texas
1863-1928

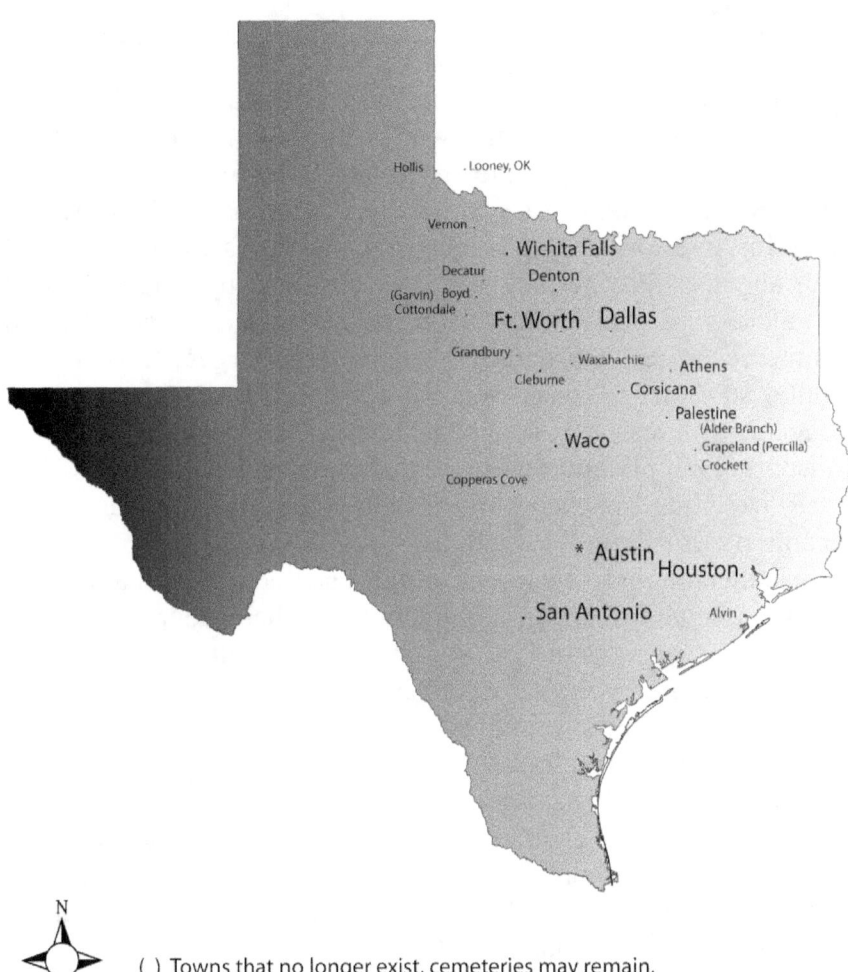

( ) Towns that no longer exist, cemeteries may remain.

Chapter 13

Henderson County, Texas, contained trees and woods similar to Anderson County, but the woods opened up more to allow larger areas for fields. In the spring the fields wore a blanket of yellow wildflowers. Creeks, rivers, and hand-dug wells provided water for livestock and farming, and the farms often contained more acreage because they were not confined by dense woods.[1] As Palestine, Texas, in Anderson County was a major mail and commerce center, the county seat, and the largest town in the county, so Athens, Texas, was the same for Henderson County. Stagecoach lines and riverboat traffic on the Trinity River transported people and goods throughout this area of Texas. The roads were hard-packed dirt except when it rained and they became rivers of mud.[2]

Henderson and Anderson Counties shared a rich Spanish and Indian heritage, reflected predominantly in their older settlements and forts. Only twenty years before, the citizens had been fighting Indians, worrying about independence from Spain, and eventually celebrating statehood.[3] This Spanish and Indian influence existed in almost every county in Texas, and it had been present in Louisiana to some extent as well, along with the French and Creole influences. Thus the Jordans were accustomed to living in communities with people from many different backgrounds. They and John and Margaret Jane Ferguson settled into the new community and proceeded to farm and raise livestock as this was their usual occupation.

Young Martha Jordan sent a note to her sister Lizzie Jordan Squyres in 1867 asking to come for a visit. John Ferguson was planning a trip back to Alder Branch in Anderson County, and Martha was hoping to create an opportunity for the family to be together again and for her to have a visit with friends at Alder Branch.

July 12, 1867
State of Texas, County of Henderson
Mrs. M.E. Squyres and Mr. H. Squyres
Dear brother and sister,

It is with the greatest of pleasure that I communicate myself to address you with a few lines to let you know that I am well at this time and hoping these few lines may come safe to hand and find you both well. I want to see you very bad. I could tell you a heap if I could see you. You might both come home with John. He is coming down there. If you will, I will go home with you if I can. I must come to a close. Nothing more at present. Fondly I remain your sister until death.

Goodbye for this time.

M.A. Jordan

Later on in the next year, March 1868, John received a letter from his cousin, Daniel Huddleston, who was a bachelor still living in the Alder Branch area where the Huddleston home place was.

State of Texas
Anderson County
March 3, 1868
Dear cousin,

I this morning have seated myself to try to write you a few lines in answer to your letter which I received and read with the greatest of pleasure. I was glad to hear from you and to hear that you and family was well. I would have been very glad to have been at some of your fine parties. I think I could of enjoyed myself finely but as I was not there to participate in your parties, it can't be helped, but I only hope that you all enjoyed yourselves as well at your parties as I did at ours. We have had dead oodles of fun here since Christmas. We can have a party whenever we want it but I think we will quit for a spell now and go to work. Well John, I wish I could see you now. I think we could have some old fun. I believe that we both can talk better than we can write.

Our layout of connection is all well as far as I know. Tom

Holdeman got into a little scrape by stealing a clevis [a U-shaped piece of iron with holes in the ends through which a pin is run to attach one thing to another] from a old nigger, and so his layout has moved back to Nacogdoches, and by that means we have got shed of some of our bulliest connection, that is bully ain't it. Well John, I was sorry to hear that you had not had any cold weather up there to save your meat, but I expect you was sorty low. You didn't have much to save unless you got it by the slight of hand.

Well John, the time of the year has come for farming, and if you have not commenced, it is high time that you was at it. The people here has been planting here for a month. They are generally done or nearly so. Lots of those old fellows up about town has got corn knee high and are separating out their cotton. That's bully ain't it. As for me, I consider myself too nice a man to follow farming. I am a going to drive oxen myself this year and then I am going to follow merchandizing or some other lumber business such as cleaning out horse stables and the like or else I will make some man's gal quake and tremble.

John, you never said a single word about my old skylark in your letter. I would like you to write to me how she is getting along and whether she is dead or not, not that I am taking on at all, but I would like to hear from her once more. I told your mother's folks what you said about them not writing and they all say they have wrote to you since they got a letter from you two on their times. Les [his brother Lewis P.] has been going down in Houston County two or three times, the boys says to see a girl, but I don't know whether it is so or not and if it is, I don't suppose he will do much harm by it.

So I will come to a close. Write to me as soon as you receive this letter. So no more only I remain as ever

D.C. Huddleston

At the time of this letter, Daniel was obviously a bachelor who enjoyed the community entertainments around Alder Branch and was young enough to be lighthearted about working and earning a living. He did not have to support a family, so he could afford to work at whatever he pleased and whenever he pleased. He may have been running with a wild crowd because apparently one of his acquaintances was not afraid of getting into trouble with the law. During the Reconstruction period in America, it had become against the law to steal from a black man, quite a departure from previous years. Parties were great fun for Dan because he was not tied down to one girl. However, he was interested in some young lady connected to or known by John Ferguson, but he asked about her in an offhand manner so as not to arouse the interest of his cousin. He did not want to be teased about his attraction. This young lady was probably Margaret Jane's younger sister, Martha, who was fast approaching marriageable age. A few months later in August, John and Margaret Ferguson received another letter from Anderson County, this time from the Squyres.

August 15, 1868
Anderson County, Texas
Mr. J.T. Ferguson and wife
Dear brother and sister,

I seat myself to write you a few lines to let you know how we are. Those lines leave us all unwell. We have all been sick since you was here. I have had the chills ever since you was here. I have just got up from a severe spell of the fever. I am so nervous that I can't hardly write. Leizy [Mary Elizabeth Jordan Squyres] has had a severe spell of the fever. She had the fever for eight days before it cooled and she is not stout yet and our poor little babe has had the worst time of us all. It [probably William Fletcher Squyres] has been sick for six weeks. It is now having the chills. When it was taken sick, it could push a chair and walk after it and could stand alone, but now it can't hardly stand or sit alone. Hoping these few lines may come to hand and find you all well. I have nothing to write of much importance. There is a great deal of sickness here and several deaths. Buck Huddleston lost one of his children. Ben Easley has lost one child recently and a good deal more about in the neighborhood.

Perry has been at my house for nine or ten days. He left today. He has gone back to Limestone County. He was well with the exception of sore eyes. He had been off with a drove of beeves and stopped on his return back. He said he did not know when he would come home. He said he expected to make another trip to Alexander with beeves before he went home. I have offered my cotton for sale but have not sold yet. My cotton is very good. Cotton is generally very fair. It bids fair at this time. The worms is in this county and is eating the cotton clean as they go. If I can sell my crop we intend to move to that county, but if I have to gather my cotton, it will be so late that I don't know whether we will move or not.

You must excuse us for not writing you before now, but we have a lawful excuse from the fact that have not been able to visit you all nor no one else since you was here. But when old master says that we are able or gives us health at any rate, we will visit you all. Perry stayed at your mother's last night. They was all well and getting along very well. There was nothing new occurred since you left here.

I will close for this time. You must write to us so nothing more only I remain yours as ever.

H. Squyres

The illness that Harmon Squyres described in his letter was just another example of the way life was in the 1800s. People had little natural resistance to fevers, and they had no effective cure for these fevers until the much later advent of penicillin. This drug, along with better sanitary conditions and more care in the handling and preparation of food would make a large difference in people's health after the turn of the century. Apparently the fever the Squyres family and others in the neighborhood had, although unnamed, was serious. The Squyres, by this time, had a son, William Fletcher, born in late 1867, and he was probably the sick child mentioned in the letter. William survived to adulthood, so he recovered from this particular bout of illness, but he was lucky and so were his mother and father. Many were not so fortunate.

Perry Jordan was old enough in 1868 to be supporting himself by working on cattle drives as a drover. The cattle industry was one of the first to recover after the war, and it offered an occupation for returning soldiers and others seeking work. A few years before, Perry had been put in charge of caring for his brothers' horses after his brothers left home to serve in the Civil War, and now he was putting his expertise with horses to good use. Perhaps he was even riding one of his brothers' horses. Although he was away from Henderson County for long periods of time while trailing cattle, he was living the life of an American folk hero, the cowboy. A common complaint of cowboys working the trail drives, however, was sore eyes from all the dust the cattle stirred up. This is why cowboys wore scarves around their necks to put over their noses and mouths, but they couldn't cover their eyes. Perry had just returned from a cattle drive, complaining of sore eyes, had spent some time with his sister's family, the Squyres, and had probably renewed old acquaintances in the Alder Branch area. He had stayed the night with John Ferguson's mother and could report that the Ferguson family was not ill and doing well.

Perry Lafayette Jordan

By the fall of 1868, John and Margaret Ferguson had decided to move back to Alder Branch and Anderson County where John's family was.[4] John never seemed to be content to be away from Anderson County for very long, and therefore, all of his children were born at Alder Branch. On October 4, 1868, his second son, John D., was born.[5] Although the Squyres had talked of moving to Henderson County in their letter of August 15, 1868, if their corn crop could be harvested, apparently they did not move that fall perhaps because John and Margaret moved first, back to Anderson County. During the next year while the Fergusons were settling back into life in the Alder Branch area, a Jordan in Henderson County had decided to make a change in her life. On December 7, 1869, Margaret Jane's younger sister, Martha Ann, married John Ferguson's cousin, Daniel C. Huddleston, in Henderson County at the Jordan home. H. E. Calahan, magistrate, presided over the ceremony.[6] Bachelor Dan was settling down. The relationship the two young people shared had grown over several years and had finally resulted in marriage. Now William and Martha Jordan had only the two youngest sons left at home, and Perry was gone much of the time working cattle drives.

Martha Ann Jordan Huddleston
In Later Years

Shortly before 1870, another family change took place. William and Martha and their two sons were joined in Henderson County by Martha Jordan, Wyatt Jordan's wife, and her children.[7] Martha had finally become convinced that a move was necessary. In 1869, Wyatt Jordan's estate was finally settled in Bienville Parish, Louisiana, and during this process, one piece of land was sold with the proceeds going to the Jordan children.[8] Martha then only had to sell the rest of the land, and the family could move. Although Louisiana was home, it was just too broken to hold much future for her children, and so she sadly packed up the family and followed her brother-in-law to Texas, hoping for something better. Her oldest daughter Caroline was married by this time to William Jefferson Guy and had two children, and Juliann was married to John Murphey and had two children.[9] The whole group moved to Texas together. At long last, the William and Wyatt Jordan families were back together again, and the reunion was permanent as they would continue to live close to one another off and on for the rest of their lives.[10] They might or might not ever find prosperity in the vast new country of Texas, and they would undoubtedly have difficulty adjusting to this different new place, but now they would have their family close.

Chapter 14

After the Civil War ended, friends of the Jordans wrote to Margaret Jordan Ferguson describing the Reconstruction years in Bienville Parish, Louisiana.

To Mrs. Maggie J. Ferguson
Dear Maggie,

I hardly know how to address you. You have been silent so long but I have found out your hiding place and I was determined to write to you and stir up your memory once more. Mag, I have often wondered why you forgotten me and never would write to me anymore. I received a letter from your sister Elizabeth some time ago. She asked me to write to her but very careful not to tell me where to direct a letter so I could not answer it. I hope she will write again.

Maggie, I am living where Mr. Stark used to live though quite a different looking place now. I must tell you something about my little family. Mag, I have the prettiest and the best young man in the country, that you know without telling - you have seen him a many a time. I have a little girl going on five years just as pretty and smart as she can be - black eyes. Her name is Catherine Victoria. My little boy is fifteen months old - blue eyes, fair complected. I am very uneasy about him. I fear I shall lose him. He is sick and has been a good while. His name is William Lewis. You must tell me about your little chaps.

Lizzie asked me about the Bates girls. Melissa married a Mr. Weeks. She lives about Campti [small town in the Red River area of northwestern Louisiana]. She had twins the first time - both boys - one did not live long, the other died five or six months ago. She had a daughter the last I heard from her. Dora is living with her. Dan and Henry are both married. Leathe has joined the church and dresses finer than any lady in the country. Mag, we are to have an association here at Carolina church next year. We have had some glorious revivals, many added to our number.

Elder John Baron is our minister. Mag, Tommy and Lewis are fine looking boys. Tom is nearly grown. Cap, the youngest one, is in bad health. Pa remains a widower yet and I expect will as long as he lives. He says he knows something about stepmothers and never will put one over Kate. She is a very small woman. Pa is building here at the church for health and I expect will put up a stone there. Uncle Andrew Babers lives where grandfather used to live. He has a large family. He has two sons about grown and a daughter.

Mag, you would be surprised to see how this country is settled up with Negroes. They are peaceable good Negroes so far. The widow Pennelia Babers is back from Texas and very anxious to marry but there is none of that going on any more. I think there will be a great many old maids. Pa has her to support. She has two hale-looking, young brothers here, but they won't do anything for her. Tell me all about your good old ma and pa - how they are getting along. I have no mother to go to see. You don't know how it pains me to think about it and the way we had to give her up. I reckon you have heard all about it.

Well Mag, I shall begin to close my letter for this time and when I hear from you I will write again. Mag, I fear you will never make out my letter. It is written so bad. I am out of practice. I have the third day fever. My hand trembles. My baby is taken the chill now. Remember me to all the family. So farewell for awhile.

Your devoted friend,
Mattie J. Holman

Mattie Holman was the former Mattie Babers who had written to Margaret Jane Jordan in Texas before either of the girls was married to tell about Mattie's loss of her fiancé in the Civil War. At that time Mattie was sure her life was over, but apparently she received a second chance at happiness, and she took it. She married James Holman who served in the same company as the Jordan boys in the Civil War and was well known to the Jordan family. Other women were not so fortunate and encountered real difficulty finding a husband because most of the men of the parish were either killed in the war or had moved away. There is no explanation as to why the Jordan girls did not communicate with Mattie, but the separation of their families by time and space certainly contributed. Everyone was busy building new lives, and as time passed, old associations in faraway places were difficult to maintain.

This letter revealed some of the societal changes in Bienville Parish, Louisiana, and some of the movement of people that characterized the South during Reconstruction. People whom the Jordans had known had died or moved to new locations, young people had grown up and married, and new children had been born. There were many more black people living in the old neighborhood, and the farms and homesteads that the Jordans had known were inhabited by different people. A few people who had moved away decided to move back, but this was not common. Life had gone on in spite of the war's devastation, but not without many differences. A letter written a few years later to Margaret Jane from a cousin who lived at Friendship in Bienville Parish went into more detail about the changing population in the parish.

June
Friendship
Bienville Parish, Louisiana
Mrs. M.J. Ferguson,

Kind friend, your kind and welcome letter is at hand and has been read with much interest by several of your old friends. Well, Margaret, you know not how much pleasure it gave us to hear from you. I will give you all the news I can think of, but if I could be with you a few days, I could tell you a heap more than I can write. Well, I will commence by telling you about myself and family. Mr. Bishop got home in the fall after the surrender and bought our old place back. He built over near Burnt Cobbin, and has got 30 acres of land cleared. We have seven children living and three dead. Nannie is in very bad health. Miss Hamitt still lives. Isaac lives here at his place where you left him. Leeler and Kate both married. Leeler married a man by the name of Morgan. Kate married Will Jones, and Bill Frey lives on your old place. He has built a little mill just below your old spring on the branch. They have 10 children living. Margaret, you would not know this country here. Since you left here, there are very few of the old settlers here that were here when you left.

There has been a large church house built at Friendship and a Masonic Hall over it. The new house stands right on the node in that little field of Malone's, and Loualin Barron has got a fine store house there and a steam mill and gin will be running in a few days. Old Brush Valley is no more. That country is all filled up with Negroes. The Grays and Fotses are all gone or dead. Liberty Hill's the place of business now in that country. There is three dry goods stores and two grocery stores. Amos Shively lives on his old place. Les Shively lives at Liberty Hill. Catherine Shively lives at Jessy M.'s old place. Jessy has gone to Mississippi. The old man and old lady Blackwood is both dead and Dave Ricks (Jolls) son lives on their old place. Les Shively married Julie Ricks. All the girls that you left here is married.

William Babers lost his wife soon after the war. Martha [Mattie Babers Holman] married J.A. Holman and their oldest daughter is grown. Dr. Gage and Colonel Walker went to Texas soon after the surrender. N.H. Bradley is clerking for L.G. Barron. Miss Harriet Fry and John Readhimer is gone to South Carolina on a visit and will be gone for two months. We have a new church house right where old Squire Bradley used to live. It belongs to the Methodists and Cumberland Presbyterians. They both have organized churches there, and we have a good school going on there now.

James Holman lives on the John Starks old place. Starks moved to the lower part of the state several years ago. Bates has moved below Nachitoches. The old man James Willson is dead and his widow is married again. Forrest Whitley's wife is dead and he had gone to Arkansas. Mrs. McCathan has gone to Desoto Parish. Her daughter married Fonso Raborn (Samp's son). The Lyons are all dead or gone.

Well, Margaret, it is a dissatisfying time here now. We ain't making more than a third of a crop of corn upon the cause of the dry weather and cotton is suffering now for rain. Margaret, I would be very glad to see you and your children but if we never meet any more on this Earth, I hope we will meet in heaven where parting will be no more. I have three little children in heaven and I am resolved to see them in heaven God being my helper. I must close for this time hoping to hear from you soon. Mr. Bishop and children all join me in sending you our best wishes.

Ever your friend and cousin,
Francis C. Bishop

This letter gives some insight into what happened to the Confederate soldiers who returned home from the Civil War. In some cases like the Bishops and the Holmans, the man was able to buy back his land or someone else's, gather up his family, and start building a life and a future. Some of the men, examples being the doctor and the captain of this account, went on to Texas and started new lives. Some went to Mexico and as far south as South America to try to escape living under Yankee rule, and a few stayed in those locations, but many returned eventually either to the South or to the West.[1] Each soldier had to find his own way back to a normal life in the chaos of Reconstruction. Some never did.

The population of Friendship in Bienville Parish as pictured in Francis Bishop's letter had changed, as had the population described in Mattie Holman's letter. Many of the former residents were dead, some had moved further west to Texas and beyond, and new people had moved into the parish. The Negroes were living in their own homes and supporting themselves, although not in any grand style. Property had exchanged hands, and different people were living on the land that used to belong to familiar family names. Very few seemed to be living in the same place as they did before the war, and most people were either stricken with poverty or making do with only a little more than subsistence living. The situation was exactly as William Jordan had predicted when he was arguing with his wife, Martha, in 1863 about moving to Texas. Their friends were scattered to the four winds, and the neighborhood was not the same. It would have done no good for the Jordans to stay in Brush Valley in 1863 because change was inevitable. The war and its aftermath very effectively ended the life that they had known there.

New buildings were constructed and new businesses started. The center of business had shifted from Brush Valley, which was practically gone, to Liberty Hill, which was growing in the number of its shops, schools, and churches. New associations and opportunities were rising from the remains of what had existed before the war. Although a few of the people who had left the South during the war or shortly thereafter eventually returned, the places they returned to were not the same as the ones they had known. People were picking up the pieces, but it would be a long struggle back to even low income levels, and one fact would remain unchanged. Family members and friends had been separated forever.

Camp Moore, the old camp in the pines at Tangipahoa, Louisiana, where the Jordan boys had gone into the army and been trained, had been completely destroyed in 1864 by Union troops. All that remained of the camp was the cemetery with its six or seven hundred graves containing the remains of the recruits who died of disease without ever facing the enemy. A quiet peace had descended upon the land where thousands of young men had camped and trained, waiting to meet their destiny on the battlefields of the Civil War. Years later, the site with its cemetery was preserved as a state historic place, and through contributions by private groups, a museum and appropriate monuments were erected in memory of the dead. When the state could no longer support the site, the private groups cared for it and solicited donations from the public for its support.[2]

At Brookhaven, Mississippi, when Gray Jordan died in 1863, he left modest holdings to be divided among his wife, children, and grandchildren. The estate was valued at around five thousand dollars with 440 acres of land, buildings and holdings, livestock and crops. It took ten years to settle the estate, and in the final 1874 settlement after the war, Gray's second wife, Nancy, received 160 acres, the home, and the farm buildings for herself and Gray's youngest children. This was the usual practice in probate settlements and was referred to as a dower for the surviving widow. She was married again by this time to a Wainwright. The rest of the estate went to Gray's other children in Mississippi who were by this time living independently on their own land and raising their own families.[3] If William Jordan was a part of the settlement, he probably sold his part to his brothers and sisters because he never returned to Mississippi.

The years after the Civil War produced hard times as the Brookhaven area struggled to rebuild. Brookhaven had been raided and burned several times during the war because it had served as a training facility for Confederate troops, the railroad had been destroyed, and the roads leading into Brookhaven were unusable because the bridges had been burned. Most of the damage had been done in 1863, first by the Union Colonel Grierson on his lightning quick and highly destructive raid through Mississippi in May and followed in July by Major Fullerton's assault on Brookhaven.[4] Of Grierson's raid, Major General U.S.Grant said, "He had spread excitement throughout the State, destroying railroads, trestle-works, bridges, burning locomotives and railway stock, taking prisoners, and destroying stores of all kinds. To use the expression of my informant, 'Grierson has knocked the heart out of the State.'"[5]

After the war, all of Brookhaven's damage had to be repaired or rebuilt and a bankrupted commerce and business district restored. The money and credit situation did not help in accomplishing this quickly. Confederate money was worthless, and the banks were having difficulty staying in business. The cotton fields were laid waste from fighting and neglect, the livestock was gone, and people's homes were in a bad state of repair. Citizens were stripped of their rights by the harsh measures of Reconstruction. However, there was money to be made in lumber and farming as soon as the transportation systems could be rebuilt, and this would be the salvation of many families. The citizens of the Brookhaven area worked hard to return to normalcy quickly and move forward, and the return of the railroad along with massive amounts of Yankee dollars helped immensely.[6] Gray Jordan's surviving children, James, Simeon, Gray, Jr., Wilson, Martha Sutton, Malinda Bardwell, Mary Ann Hickman, and Sarah worked at farming, milling, and in the lumber industry, and they managed fairly well, but they were never as comfortable again as they had been before the war.[7] Nevertheless, they were able to provide enough for themselves and to nurture the next generation of Jordans. Most of them lived to be elderly and had large families. Some moved to Louisiana, and some stayed in Mississippi.

Brookhaven's Railroad Station

With the rebirth of the railroad came new people and businesses to the Brookhaven area and economic recovery. These fresh influences resulted in a new county being formed in 1870 named after former President Abraham Lincoln with Brookhaven as the county seat. Much of the land taken for the new county came from Lawrence County which was greatly reduced in size. Whether there was resentment by the old-time citizens at all these changes hardly mattered. Lincoln County was bustling with activity and on the move towards a better future.[8] And yet, there would always be a sadness among those who had served the Confederacy and come home to rebuild their county and state. When Simeon Jordan, William Jordan's younger brother, died in 1927, an old friend and comrade, A.M. Summers, complimented Simeon on always being a good, dependable citizen in war and peace and remarked, "At the services I was made to feel, not so sorrowful for the departed one, for Sim had lived to a good old age, but when I looked around and saw that I was the only Confederate soldier present and one of the same company that he belonged to, and remembering that there were only four of us left, I was sad and lonesome."[9]

In Texas, the Jordans were surviving Reconstruction by moving to new areas where the prospects for farming and ranching were better. Texas had not suffered the destruction that the rest of the Southern states had although cash and credit were still hard to come by. However, the land was vast and free, full of possibilities, and always calling to William's restless spirit. If William had ever intended to establish a homeplace in one location and watch it grow and prosper, the Civil War had changed his ability and drive to do that. Nevertheless, he and his children, although always eager to move on, were strong enough to survive. They were not afraid of hard work, their needs were simple, and their sense of humor was a constant buffer against pain and disappointment. They believed in themselves and in God's ability to take care of them.

Chapter 15

Around 1870, Harmon and Mary Elizabeth Squyres and their family decided to move to Henderson County, Texas to be near her parents, William and Martha Jordan. They did not have enough money to buy land, but they lived near the Jordans with a Miss Call, and Harmon may have worked for William and others as a hired laborer and carpenter. The following letter was written by Lizzie Squyres back to her sister Margaret in Anderson County. Juliann (Julia) Murphey, a cousin who was the daughter of Wyatt and Martha Jordan, wrote a note on the back of the letter. Julia, along with the rest of Wyatt's family, was living near the Squyres and Jordans in Henderson County at that time, having just moved from Louisiana.

December 21, 1873
Henderson County, Texas
Mr. J.T. and Mrs. M.J. Ferguson
Dear brother and sister,

It is with the greatest of pleasure that I seat myself to write you a few lines to let you know that I have not forgotten you. This is an answer to your kind letter. Those few lines leave us all in moderate health. I hope when those few lines come to hand, they may find you all enjoying good health. Dear sister, I am very sorry that your feelings was so badly hurt with me. Maggie, I assure you that I never got a letter from you but what I answered promptly. I don't know the reason that you didn't get my letter. I wrote to you the same time I wrote to Mat. Ma and Pa had one letter sent back to them. They say some would take them out of the office. Dear Maggie, I hope you will continue to write. I will try to be as prompt as my word. Well I don't know that I can write anything that will interest you this time. I have wrote all particulars in Mat's letter. You will get it all. Harmon went to preaching church today. There wasn't no preaching so we wondered what sort of a preacher we will have this year until the third sabbath in January. I must close for this time. I want to write to Perry tonight. I will close by asking an interest in your prayers.

M.E. Squyres

On the back of ME Squyres letter of December 21, 1873
From Henderson Co., Texas
Mat Huddleston and Margaret Ferguson,

Dear cousin, it is with pleasure that I take my pen in hand to write you a few lines to let you know that I have not forgotten you though I have been careless about writing. I hope you will excuse me and I will try to do better the next time. This leaves me in bad health. I have a chill Thursday and this one. The rest of the family is well. I hope when these few lines reach you, they may find you all well. I haven't got no news of interest to write. Times is hard, and money is scarce. You must excuse my short letter for this time. You must write to me. I will come to a close by asking an interest in your prayers to almighty God, and if we meet no more on this earth, I hope we may meet in heaven where pain and parting will be known no more.

Julia A. Murphey

These letters contained a lot of apologizing. Letter writing in the 1800s was thought to be an important obligation, so if it was judged to be poorly done, the writer felt obliged to apologize. This convention was probably taught in school or by parents who instructed their children in letter writing. Another convention seemed to be that the Jordans and others of this time period felt that they didn't have anything "important" to write to each other most of the time. On the contrary, the facts of their everyday lives were important to their relatives who loved to get letters as a means of entertainment and reassurance that family members were all right. Even if the news in the letters was not good, at least it was better than not knowing anything.

Lizzie's letter recounted another instance of a letter lost in the mail. Even though the war was over, the mail was still unreliable, and apparently, it was even stolen out of the post office. Besides the deplorable state of the mail, Julia's letter revealed two more conditions of Reconstruction life in Texas - ill health and poverty. The Jordan women living under the hardships of 1870 were quite different from the young girls who wrote to each other during the Civil War. These young girls had grown into women of strength, resigned to enduring less than ideal living conditions while raising their families. Only in their humor and laughter could anyone still see the shadow of what they had been when they were young. What would their lives have turned out to be if there had been no Civil War in America? Would they have married the local neighborhood boys and eventually been well off or at least comfortable, building upon what their parents had started? There was, of course, no way of knowing that, and they had no time to speculate on it. Committed to making the best of their present situation and finding happiness and fulfillment where they could, they could not afford to live in the past. All of the Jordan cousins, Margaret Jane, Lizzie, Martha, Julia Ann, and Caroline, lived to be elderly and raised large families in Texas. This was a testament to their endurance and acceptance of life as it came.

The realization that death was an ever- present reality was still evident in the closing of every letter to friends or family, even in this post-war period. Not only was it a letter-writing convention to close this way, but it expressed a belief in the way life was. An example of this is included in the following letter from the Squyres to the Huddlestons.

December 21, 1873
Henderson County, Texas
D.H. and M.A. Huddleston
Dear brother and sister,

It is with much pleasure that I seat myself this sabbath morning to answer your kind letter. I was very sorry to hear that you was all in bad health. We have all had moderate health this fall so far. Emer [Lizzie Squyres's daughter Margaret Emma who would have been six] had the third day chills about two weeks. She has quit having the chills though she has a slight fever. I think the next time she will make it. If you was to see her, you wouldn't think that she was sick and the family is well now. Ma looks better than she has in a long time. Mr. Guy [Caroline Jordan's husband] and his family and Emily and the two children [all children of Wyatt and Martha Jordan] is all gone to Bosque County [Texas]. We got a letter from them last week. They thought they would like that country very well if they could have good health. They said everybody looked well out there. Julie [Jordan Murphy] and John is here with me. They don't know where they will go. Julie is not well. She has been having the chills about one week. I hope she will get them stopped. Well, Mat, I have got one good word to write. We have moved from Miss Call's. We live on the improvement that Perry made [prospective landowners could make improvements on land and then have first claim on ownership of it]. We don't know whether we will stay here or not. If we can buy the land, we will stay here. I reckon we will know next week. The land belongs to Mr. Martin. Mr. Martin and Mr. Micham divided this league. There is plenty of land in this country now for sale. There is several moved in here this fall. I wish you would all come to see us this winter. If we buy this place we won't have time to come down there. Well, I do not know what more I can write this time. You must write to me often. If I live, I expect to come to see you all sometime. Write some and often. So I must close my short letter by asking an interest in your prayers to our heavenly father. If we never more meet on earth, we may meet in heaven where pain and parting is no more.

M.E. Squyres

Dear brother and sister,

I will write you a few lines. That is if I can think of anything to write. I am well but my hand and that is very sore. It is so sore that I can't hardly write. Lizzy stated that we had moved to the place that Perry started to improve on Clear Creek. I will buy the land if I can get it. The land now belongs to Major Martin. He is at Palestine at this time attending court. Dan, I received your order to Willson. I will do the best I can. If I get the land, I will secure your money. I have nothing to write that would interest you any at all. Paten Bond and Ad Smith has lately married. There is such talk as Lucinda Etheride and Frank McMan is marrying this week. Excuse these few lines.

H. Squyres

William J. and Caroline Jordan Guy

Daniel and Martha Jordan Huddleston were living near John and Margaret Jane Ferguson at Alder Branch in Anderson County. Daniel's and John's families were still located in this area as well.[1] Any letter written to the Huddlestons was shared with John and Margaret and vice versa to get family news passed along. This letter from the Squyres in Henderson County had news of Wyatt Jordan's family. The Guys and Murpheys, Wyatt Jordan's two daughters' families, had moved away from William and Martha Jordan and out to Bosque County which was farther west in Texas where the air was drier and the land more open and healthy. This would not be their final move. Both William and Wyatt Jordan's families would move many more times in the years that followed, sometimes living near each other, sometimes not.[2] They all seemed to be afflicted with the same restlessness, the same desire to keep looking for a better place. Bosque County would fit the needs of Wyatt's family for now, but not for long.

Although the Squyres had intentions of buying the land on Clear Creek, there are no records that show that they did. They did have another child, Margaret Emma, born in 1867. Daniel and Martha had three sons by 1875: William Newton born in 1870, Perry Lee born in 1872, and Daniel C. Jr. born in 1874. Margaret Jane and John Thomas Ferguson had two more sons: K. Danny born in July of 1870 and Thomas Floyd born in 1875.[3]

The number of William and Martha Jordan's grandchildren was growing steadily. The number of their unmarried children, however, was decreasing. On December 7, 1872, Perry married Mary Ann "Molly" Dean in Cherokee Co., Texas, where her family was living.[4] He may have met her when his family first moved to Texas or later while working on one of his cattle drives.

Mary Ann Dean was the daughter and only child of Drury Dean and Clementine Cordelia Fondren. Drury Dean died around 1853, and Clementine had other children by a second marriage to William Posey. According to her descendants in the Perry Jordan family, Mary Ann may have had Native American blood (Cherokee or Choctaw) through her mother or her father or both.[5] Cherokee County as a whole had a rich heritage in Native American culture and history.[6] However, Mary Ann's mother had emigrated to Cherokee County with her family, the Fondrens, from Lawrence County, Mississippi, another area of the country rich in Native American history and also the home county of the William H. Jordans.[7] Perry had been born in that county in Mississippi. Whether the Jordans and Fondrens had known each other in Mississippi is not known. After his marriage, Perry remained in Cherokee County, but he started farming rather than working as a cowboy on the cattle drives. Married life meant settling down. His marriage left only one child still at home with William and Martha, their last child, William C. or "Billy" as family members called him.

Mary Ann Dean Jordan in Later Years

By this time, William and Martha were doing fairly well in Henderson County with two hundred acres of land and a small amount of stock.[8] The more wide-open country in that county agreed with them, and their health was good for a change. It was the first time they had lived in country that was not heavily forested and swampy, and they were not as troubled by fevers caused by insects and high humidity. However, by 1876, changes were coming for all the family members.

Chapter 16

Perry and Mary Ann Jordan's first child, Floyd Gilbert was born in 1875.[1] Perry, his sister Martha, and his sister Margaret Jane remembered their brothers who had been lost in the Civil War by naming sons after them. Because Perry carried the Jordan name, his son's name was almost exactly the same as his brother's. In this way, a part of the boys who had died so young lived on. The following letter was written to John and Margaret Ferguson by Perry and Mary Ann Jordan early in 1876.

February 29, 1876
Jacksonville, Cherokee Co., Texas
Mr. and Mrs. Ferguson
Dear brother and sister,

It is with the greatest of pleasure that I endeavor to write you a few lines to let you know that I haven't forgotten you all. These few lines leaves us all well at the present, hoping when these lines come to hand, they may find you all enjoying the same part of God's blessings.

Mr. Jordan is planting corn. He commenced the 25th. He is not a going to plant only cotton. He is going to plant all corn. Mr. Jordan is plowing. His mare that he got from Mr. John Delaney she has took two spells of kicking. Well Margaret, I have got all of my garden planted. My peas and mustard is up.

Well, I must tell you something about our boy. He is sitting alone. Well Margaret, he is larger than your boy was when you was over here. I reckon you think that we don't intend to ever come to see you, but if we can find a little time, we are going to come to see you all. Well, times is hard and prospects is for harder. Well we haven't heard from Henderson since Christmas. Write soon.

Mary Ann Jordan

Dear brother and sister,

A few words in addition to Molly's letter. Our grange is a working to grow and is going to work through committees which may be a great advantage. We are going to quit raising so much cotton and try to raise more small grains. I am going to try my hand at corn and peas and potatoes and rye and oats for the present year.

John, we thought we would come to see you and Margaret Jane fine through the winter but I ran out of time. Though, we will come sometime soon. I would like to converse with you. I want you and Dan to be ready to go with me to the prairies next summer and look us out a home so truly we can make something. Well, come and see us when you can and write when you can't.

Perry L. Jordan

These letters reflected the hard times which existed in Texas after the Civil War, but they also told of the new ideas that farmers were willing to embrace in order to regain pre-Civil War prosperity. Through these years the Jordans were constantly trying to improve their situation by moving to new locations, trying new methods of farming and ranching, or trying new occupations. As well as being a farmer/rancher, Perry worked as a preacher in Cherokee County, whether through a church or part time as a fill-in is not known.[2] Of greatest importance, farmers were getting away from planting cotton as their only crop. It was hard on the soil, and the cotton market remained highly unpredictable after the war. Cotton was still king in Texas, but crop rotation was increasing in popularity. The growth of the Grange organization for farmers also impacted the development of new ways of farming and ranching. Grange meetings were excellent places to hear about the latest agricultural ideas and compare notes with other farmers and ranchers. The Grange also had the potential to become a political vehicle for obtaining favorable legislation for farmers from the state and federal government. However, this did not come to fruition in the 1870s.[3] The exploratory visit to the prairies that Perry refers to may never have occurred, but if it did, it might have encouraged the William Jordans to move west later in the summer. However, it did not affect Perry's situation because, according to government records, Perry and his family stayed in Cherokee County until around 1880 when they moved to Navarro County.[4]

William C. "Billy" Jordan

In April of 1876, the last of William and Martha's children, William C., married Sarah Frances Simmons at her father's house in Navarro Co.[5] William could have been living by himself by this time and working in Navarro County as a laborer or ranch hand where he met Frances. He was around 20 years old, old enough to be living away from home. Known by at least some of the family members as "Billy," he was the baby of the family and considerably younger than his older sisters. His turn had finally come to marry and have a family of his own.

In 1876 William decided it was time to move again, even though he was doing fairly well in Henderson County. He had land and a small herd of livestock, as well as his farming operation. The new location was to the west, more than half way across Texas in Erath County where the country was much more wide open but still hilly and rocky with tree lines and thick brush. His youngest son William and his wife moved also. The Squyres did not accompany the Jordans on the move out West, but instead they stayed in Henderson County and later moved to adjoining Navarro County. Some of the members of Wyatt Jordan's family eventually moved to Navarro as well.[6] Why did William feel he had to move on? The reason is not known, but it could have been that the family felt the country in Henderson was not good for their health any longer or the land was not good enough. Lizzie Squyres wrote about the Jordans' move to Erath County to her sisters, Margaret Ferguson and Martha Huddleston, and their families at Alder Branch in late 1876.

Henderson County
November 5, 1876
Dear brothers and sisters and children,

It is through the kindnesses of God that I am alive to write you a few lines to let you know I haven't forgotten you all. It seems as though you have all forgotten us or else there is something the matter some way. I have no recollection of the last letter I received from any of you. You may have all been sick as we have. Our family has been sick ever since the last of July. There hasn't been none of us dangerously sick as I know of. Emer [her daughter Margaret Emma] had one right bad fever. We had the doctor with her one time. That is the only time we have had the doctor this year. We have got medicine several times from him. I had three or four very hard chills. I got them stopped and then I just had slow fevers for about seven weeks. I do not think the children have been sick as much as me and Harmon has.

Harmon hasn't been able to do any work this fall. He has made it out to get his corn gathered with help. Well my good sisters, our old mother and father is gone a long ways from here. They left here the last of August. They stopped in Eastland County. I received a letter from them the other day. They both got sick before they got there. Ma had got well when they wrote but Pa was not well. Billy [her brother William] and Francis was well. Pa wrote they was wonderfully pleased. He says he wouldn't come back if Pearce would give him his old place. Ma wanted to come down there very bad before she left, but she did not have anybody to come with her. We was not able to come and Pa got sick. She said she was coming back this winter, but I do not look for her. They did not say anything about it in the letter.

Well, if nothing happens, we will leave Henderson Co. before long. Harmon has rented lands in Navarro Co., within one

mile of Rice. When you write, direct your letter to Navarro Co.
Rice P.O. That is the prettiest country I ever saw and it has
proved to be a healthy country. Well Mat, we will be right in
Mitchum town again. Myself and Mary McInis and Grandma
Mitchum will all get water out of the same well. We will have
good water to drink. I want to see you all very bad, but I do not
know any chance to see you soon. If we get where we can have
good health, I hope we can visit some next year. Well, I have
wrote all I can think of this time. I will write you Pa's address:
Erath Co., Wenomia P.O. Box. Write to me soon. Goodbye.

Lizzie

Between 1876 and 1878, apparently more moves took place
in the Jordan family. The Squyres either did not move to Navarro
County around 1876, or they did and then moved back to
Henderson County briefly before going on to Hood County and
the Granbury area just prior to 1880. William and Martha Jordan
moved back from Erath County to Navarro County in this period,
and their son William and his wife Francis moved as well,
probably because Navarro County was Francis's home and
familiar territory.[7] In October of 1878, Lizzie Squyres wrote to
her sister Margaret Jane from Henderson County, Texas. She did
not have good news.

October 26, 1878
Henderson County, Texas
Dear sister and family,

It is with much pleasure that I seat myself to answer your
kind letter which I received tonight. I was mighty glad to hear
from you all once more in life. I was very sorry to hear of the
sickness you have all been having. I am glad it is no worse than it
is dear Maggie. We haven't had no great deal of bad sickness
except our dear little Travis. He is dead. He died on the 14th of
September. He was sick for weeks. He had the fever near two
weeks and lost it for a few days. He relapsed and he taken cold
and it settled in one of his lungs. I thought I could sympathize
with you before but I didn't as I can now. I thought of you all the
time. He was the biggest and fastest child you nearly ever saw.

He had just got so he could say granma sometimes. I think I never can get over his death. I always think of you. Well, Maggie, there is one great consolation if we can be so lucky as to get to heaven, we will meet our dear little ones again. I sometimes think it won't be but a little while. Emer has had one right bad spell since Travis died. She is looking as well as ever. She is salivated but not bad. She had the ulcerated sore throat. I would have written to you before now. Every time I would think of writing, I would think of my dear child. It seemed like I never could stand to write of his death.

I wish you could all come up here to see us all. Ma is in mighty bad health and has been the most of this year. She looks very bad. Her foot has been very bad. Several times this year it was right bad. The last time I saw her you know how she is. She won't take care of herself. I can't go and stay there all the time. I go every time I can. Harmon was down there the other day. She was having the fever every day I think. If you could come up, it would do her some good, Maggie. I don't know where we will be next year. We haven't got our cotton half out yet. I wish I could live close by you all. I hate to leave Ma to go anywhere while she lives. If you can come, come and see her.

Mr. Guy and his family [Wyatt Jordan's daughter Caroline's family] and Emily [Wyatt Jordan's daughter] is going west. Wilson [Wyatt Jordan's son] is done gone. Simon [Wyatt Jordan's son] says he is not going. Murphey [Wyatt Jordan's daughter Juliann's husband] is going if he can get off. They aim to start next Monday week. If Harmon don't buy a place, you need not be surprised to see us coming.

I believe I have wrote all that I can think of this time. Tell John it takes him a long time to get in the notion to write that long letter. You must all write often. I will close this letter on the 29th of October. I received a letter from Mat [Martha Huddleston] yesterday. I will write to her this evening. Tell Perry it has been a long time since I received a letter from him. Give him and Molly my love and Mat and her family and all inquiring friends. Receive a reasonable portion for you and your family. Tell Johnny [Margaret Jane's son], Freddy and Emer [Lizzie's children] hasn't forgotten him and Neuty [Martha Huddleston's son] yet. They talk about them a great deal. They talk about Aunt Maggie and Aunt Mat every day. Freddy says Ma it is time for us to go to see Aunt Maggie again. Remember me in your prayers.

M.E. Squyres

Life was always uncertain, especially in the West. Sickness was prevalent and death was an ever-present reality. Children often did not grow up to be adults, and this fact encouraged people to have many children. Readily available and dependable birth control was unheard of, but it would not have been utilized much in any case because the customs and needs of the times dictated large families. However, the continual birth of new babies in families did not make the loss of beloved children any easier to bear. Lizzie's reference to sympathy for her sister supports the idea that Margaret Jane had similarly lost young children. There is no record of two of Margaret's sons after 1878, David and K. Danny. They probably died young and were buried in graves that have since lost any markings in Ferguson Cemetery, just outside Alder Branch. This cemetery was established in the 1840s by the early Fergusons in the area, but the Huddlestons and other related families were buried here as well. Long after Alder Branch had disappeared as a town, the cemetery remained.

Ferguson Cemetery near Palestine, Texas

Lizzie's letter also seems to suggest that William and Martha Jordan had moved closer to the Squyres who were in Henderson

County. This new location was probably Navarro County, next door to Henderson, because in 1880 William and Martha and their son William and his wife Francis were living in Navarro County.[8] This county had a rich historical past, including a Spanish and Indian influence in the early years before Texas statehood and a staunchly Confederate affiliation during the Civil War. Corsicana was the county seat and largest town, but Rice was also a town of note. The country was similar to Henderson County - more wide open with rows of trees bordering the fields but no heavy, dense forest. This country was much flatter than Henderson County, however, and drained by the Trinity River. The rich, dark soil made good farm and pasture land and supported deciduous as well as evergreen trees and scrub brush.[9] Perhaps the more wide-open country was dryer and more conducive to good health. At any rate, this was Lizzie's opinion. She mentioned the fact that her family would have good water to drink if they moved there. Her reference to the well in Mitchum probably referred to a community water well or cistern common to small towns in Texas. In the letter Lizzie wrote in 1878, her mother, Martha Jordan, had been very ill even though she was living in the healthier climate of Navarro County. Lizzie was having difficulty taking care of her and seeing after her own family as well. No matter where the Jordans lived in Texas in the late 1800s, it seemed illness was a part of their lives.

In 1871, shortly before the Jordans moved there, the railroad came to Navarro County, and that helped the local economy to grow by encouraging the farmers and ranchers to find better markets for their crops and cattle.[10] Railroads were being constructed all over the Southern states in America in order to speed economic recovery. This industry was a major factor in the taming of the West as well. The railroad had also come to Palestine, Texas, in Anderson Co., and this contributed greatly to the growth of the timber industry in that county. Once the timber was harvested, it could be transported to the rest of the country.[11] This same establishment of railroads had occurred in Mississippi and Louisiana where the timber industry helped those states to begin to recover economically.

The following letter from William Jordan to his daughter

Margaret Jane may have been written from Navarro County.

No date or place

Well, we are proud to say to you that we have enjoyed extremely fine health ever since we last saw you. We now have a bad cold but not serious. We are up. Liza and Harmon and their children is well. Liza was unwell a few days ago. Well John, I was somewhat disappointed to not have seen you before now. Well, it is disheartening if it keeps on raining as it has been doing. The ground is so wet that we cannot plow more than one third of the time. It seems that we cannot get rise to the mud. We have had mud in abundance this winter and cannot get used to it, no sir.

Well, I am getting along slow at farming. I have commenced to plant corn. Harmon is planting corn. A great many are planting corn this week. Ma is gardening to some extent. She has turnips, mustard, and onions all up. Well Maggie, Ma has 40 hens. She is selling eggs.

I haven't heard of a fuss between any persons. The temperance cause is raging in this vicinity. I know something about the Knights of Temperance. Parson Young has gave two lectures at Rice on temperance. Well, I think sometimes of selling out and coming to Anderson this spring if I can make anything by selling. I am tired of the mud. Well Maggie we have three young calves. We have milk and butter at our house, and Ma has made a lot of peach pies this evening. I guess they will come on the table tomorrow morning. We wish you were all here to dine with us. Ma said that she wants to see you all as bad as ever, and she thinks that she wants to see your children worse than ever.

Well, I would like to see you all some too, but if I can't, I can write and tell you. This is a fine farming country. If it wasn't so muddy when it rains, I would fancy it. We send our respects to inquiring friends. W.H. and Martha Jordan

Written along the side of the letter: May the good Lord bless and save you all is our prayer.

William's mention of the temperance movement illustrated another societal change in America that occurred after the Civil War. Religious and community leaders became increasingly more alarmed about the numbers of people drinking alcohol to excess and the proliferation of saloons. Competition among breweries was brisk, encouraging even young children to drink spirits. Perhaps people were trying to forget the war and hard times through drinking, but the preservation of family and moral values was at stake. Temperance organizations sprang up all over the country, and their power continued to grow through the turn of the century, culminating in the eighteenth amendment to the United States Constitution outlawing the sale of alcohol. However, prohibition stimulated the growth of organized crime and gang warfare in the larger cities because there was still an active market for liquor even though it was against the law. Citizens eventually got tired of not being safe, of fearing for their lives every time they walked the streets, and of the police and justice system not being able to control the situation. Thus the eighteenth amendment was doomed to failure because in many people's view, prohibition, no matter how well-intentioned it was, just wasn't worth the trouble it caused. The prohibition movement, although it had affected politics and religious activities for many years, could not withstand the new opposition, and the eighteenth amendment was repealed. Although the amendment had failed, the prohibition movement did succeed in curbing the number of people who drank alcohol to excess. People did seem to show a little more common sense in their drinking habits.[12]

William's voice in this letter was that of a southern gentleman, even though the grammar was not up to twentieth century standards. He was raised a gentleman, and a gentleman he would remain all of his life in spite of his economic circumstances. The past, which was the old South, continued to echo through the voices of the Jordans in their letters to each other. That way of life was gone, but the people who had lived it survived still. Again, the Jordans' sense of humor, their ability to laugh at themselves and their circumstances, colored the voice in this letter.

By 1876 all of William and Martha's children were married, and in February of 1879 in Navarro County, Texas, their last child had a child of his own. William and Francis had a son,

Joseph Commodore.[13] Martha and Dan Huddleston also had a
child that year, another son who they named Louis Monroe.
Margaret Jane and John Ferguson had their first and only girl in
1877, Lanora Bell, and Perry and Mary Ann Jordan had a second
son, Drue Hendrix. In 1878, the Fergusons had another son,
James Walter.[14] The number of William and Martha's
grandchildren continued to grow even though several were lost
early in life. The year 1880 found the elder Jordans, William C.
and his family, and Perry and Mary Ann Jordan living in Navarro
County. The Squyres were living in Hood County, southwest of
Ft. Worth, along with most of Wyatt Jordan's family. Dan and
Martha Huddleston had moved to Wise County, northwest of Ft.
Worth, and Margaret Jane and John Ferguson had also moved to
Hood Co.[15] Everyone in the family seemed to have the Jordans'
itchy feet, and they were trying a new location.

Henderson County Texas   Oct 1st 2nd 18 78

Dear sister & family it is with mutch pleasure tho
I seat my self to answer your kinde letter whitch I reseiv
To night I was mity glad to here from you all once more
in life I was of very sory to here of the sickness you have
all bin having I am glad it is no worse than it is Dear
Maggie we havent had no greateale of sickness except our dear
little travis he is ded he died on the 14 ob sept he was sick foer
weakees he had the fevere near two vrake & mist it A few dayes
he relapsed he taken cold colde & it setteed one his lunges O
I thought I could simpathise with you before but I
dident as I can now I thought ofyou all the
time he was the bigist fatest childe you nerly ever saw
he had juste got so he could say granma some times I
think I'e never can get over his death I always thinck of
you well Maggie there is one great consolation if wecan
be so luckey as to get to heven we will meat our
dear little ones A gone I some times I think it wont
be but A little while ever has had one wright bad
spell sinse travis died she is looking as well as ever she
is salivated but not bad she had the ulceed
sore throte I would have writen to you before now every time
I would thinck of writing I would thinck of my Dear
childe it searred like I never could stand to write of his
death I wish you could all come up here to see you us all

ma is in writty bad helth and has bin the moste of this
year she looks ever bad hers foot has bin very bad severil
times this year it was right bad the laste time I saw hers
you no how she is she wonts take care of here self &
canste you't stay there all the time I go evry time I can
harmon was down there the other day she was having the
fever evry day I think if you could come up it would do
here some good maggie I dont no whare I we will be next
year we havent got our colten half out yet I wish I
could live closte by you all I hate to leave ma to go
eny whare while she lives if you can come come & see here
mr gy & his family & emly is going west wilson is done
gone simon says he is not going murfey is going if he
can get off they ame to stare next monday week f harmon
donte by & place you nedent be supposse to ar coming
I beliye I have wrote all that I can think of this time
tell john it & takes him a long time to get in the notion
to write that longe letter you moste all write often I
will cose this letter on the 29 of Oct I received a letter
from mat yesterday I will write to here this evening
tell perry it has bin a longe time since I received
a letter from him give him & moley my love & mat
& here family & all inqureing friendes received a several
portion for you & family tell joney feddy & emer hasnt
forgotten him and meurty yet they talk about them
a great cale they talk a bout aunt mg & aunt mat evry day
feddy sais ma it is time for us to go to se annt mag I gain remember
me in yours prayers Me & Squyres

Chapter 17

"The Jordans were pretty restless, weren't they," I concluded after listening to their story once again. "Why couldn't they settle in one place and make a success of it?"

"The only members of the family to do that were Dan and Martha Huddleston who moved to Wise County around 1880 and stayed there until they died. Even they weren't all that successful, however," Mom answered.

"Why?" I persisted.

"I think the times had a lot to do with it. It took a long time to rebuild the economy in the South, so that people could actually make some money. Also, the Civil War destroyed people's ability to know who they were and where they belonged. What little the war left intact, Reconstruction finished obliterating. People no longer had a home they could recognize, everything had changed, they were uprooted, and for many, the rest of their lives would be a search for what they had before the war. Their center had been destroyed. Instead of finding value in the place where they were and building a home there, they were always looking over the horizon to some place better. The constant 'moving on' guaranteed they would not be successful."

"Was everyone like this after the war?" I wondered.

"No," Mother replied. "Some people, for example the Jordans, probably had some natural tendencies towards restlessness and dissatisfaction with their current state of affairs, no matter how good that might be. The 'moving on' was still occurring for generations after the Civil War, indicating it had something to do with personality. This situation wasn't all bad because it contributed to the settling of the West, but it just didn't tend to make people rich.

"Do you think the Jordans were sad not to be wealthy?" I asked.

Mom thought awhile and said, "I think they were more

worried about just surviving, and I think the women in the family were often exasperated by the constant moving. However, these people had very simple needs, and they valued the love of their family and God more than anything else. They weren't sad about not being wealthy, but they always wanted to be better off than they were."

"Do you really think they would have been better off staying in one place and making a successful life there?" This was my last question before dashing off to a friend's house.

"Well, in later years, several of the properties that had been owned by the Jordans and their children proved to be very successful. Large deposits of gas, acres of timber, and the ranch and farming land itself proved to be very valuable. If they had kept the properties they owned and passed them down through the generations, who knows what would have happened. Instead, each generation had to make or try to make its own fortune or success. When I think about it, maybe that was for the best after all, and certainly, the original Jordans would not have benefitted from land which only became valuable in the future. Still, it is interesting to think about what might have happened if the Jordans had just stayed in one place," Mom concluded.

"I don't have to think about what might happen if I don't hurry up and get over to Cindy's. She is going to kill me," I predicted as I ran out the back door.

Chapter 18

Hood County, Texas, southwest of Ft. Worth, contained the Brazos River, hills, broad mesas, and flat farming country near the tree-lined river. Tree lines bordered large areas of grassland dotted with brush and bushes.[1] The area where the Squyres, Fergusons, and members of Wyatt Jordan's family settled in 1880 was around Granbury, a prosperous town located fairly close to the Brazos River. It was the county seat and could also claim a small college and an opera house. The college was reflective of the growing interest in higher education in the post-Civil War West. The citizens of Texas wanted their children to be as educated as those raised in the East, and most did not have the option of sending their children to an Eastern university because of the cost and distance involved.

The town buildings surrounding the courthouse square were built of wood originally, but gradually through the 1880s, the wood buildings were replaced with stone ones, mostly limestone. The town streets were unpaved, but were sufficient for horse and wagon travel. They were dusty, though, and when it rained, they became muddy, making the wooden sidewalks in front of the businesses a real blessing. In the 1880s the courthouse was a simple, stone edifice, but it was replaced around 1890 with a larger gray stone structure complete with steeples and a clock tower.[2]

Grandbury, Texas

Grandbury, Texas Jail

The Squyres and Jordans watched many of these changes take place as this town and the surrounding area was home to them until around the mid 1890s.[3] This country was drier than any they had known previously and more wide open. Except for periods of drought, it was healthier for them, without the insects and swampy conditions of the forested areas. However, Margaret Jane and John Ferguson did not stay long at Granbury. Late in 1880, they moved back to Houston County, a neighboring county to Anderson, and near the town of Grapeland. They were not far from Palestine and Alder Branch but in country which was not as forested and more open. The following letter written to William H. Jordan recounts the Ferguson's move.

September 17
Grapeland, Houston County, Texas
W.H. Jordan
Dear Pa and Ma,
    I will try to write you a few lines to let you know how we are getting along. We are all tolerable well. I was sick some on the road, but I stood the trip better than I expected to. I had fever two days and bothered with asthma some. I have been worse off since I stopped than I was on the road, but I am doing very well now.

Floyd's eyes is better. We got some medicine in Palestine that has helped them a great deal. We intend to start him and Nora to school next Monday. His eyes is not strong enough yet. We had some bad luck on the road. Our calves gave out or very near and we sold the cows. We got a very good horse for the bunch. Old Gin got foundered. We got her within six miles of Waxahachie and left her with Ama. We haven't heard from her yet. We got along all right from then. We were ten days on the road. We stopped at Leona's three days - got there Friday. They were meeting there. It rained Sunday and the weather looked so bad we stayed until Tuesday. We have got a house within a half mile of sis. It is a good house and fields with it. We haven't got the use of all of it, but I wouldn't know what to do with it if I had it. John is gone to try to buy the mule he was talking about. You would like to know how we like this country. That is yet in the future, and I don't know how long. It is owing to what we can do. Direct to: MJ Ferguson Grapeland

Moving was not easy. In this letter was the first mention of Margaret Jane's lung difficulties, partly due to asthma, which plagued her most of her life. This made relocating and traveling on dusty roads in an open wagon even more uncomfortable. Her son Floyd's eyes were bothered as well. If the weather turned bad and it started raining, the roads, such as they were, would turn to mud, leaving travelers hastily seeking shelter wherever they could find it. Moving was evidently hard on animals also because the Fergusons had to sell their small herd of cows and leave one horse behind with a friend on this trip. After reaching the Grapeland area, everyone seemed to recover and like the new living accommodations, but Margaret was reserving judgment on the place. And sure enough, the Fergusons apparently decided they did not like the Grapeland area in Houston County because by 1882 they were back at Alder Branch in Anderson County and receiving mail there. The Ferguson men, it seemed, never wanted to be very far away from the home place for any length of time. Although it was by no means a mansion, it was the closest thing they had to a permanent home. The following letter came from some friends, Matt and Mary Mead, during this time of moving around. They were living at a small community southeast of Palestine, Texas, called Ioni.

Ferguson Home Place in Later Years

Ioni, Texas
June 11, 1881
Mr. and Mrs. Ferguson
Dear friends,

   I seat myself tonight to drop you a few lines to let you know that we are all well. I have no news to write you more than crops look as fine as I ever seen in my life. Though cotton is in the grass I have the best crop I ever have had since I came to Texas though I have a fine grass and I am not by myself. Lim and Sims is in the same condition and I don't know of anyone that is not in the grass. The health of the country is good. There has not been but one or two deaths. Dr. Woodara's lady died last Tuesday. John, Ioni is still ahead as to the Providence church trials. They worked on Mulin's trial until they fizzled out and threw a rope at Z.R. Harben. He went to Jim Monkes's and wanted some grouse from the lady so I have been informed by Jim himself. So you remember the Petterson case. He says he can beat this. They have not brought it into the church yet though. They will next conference. You had better come down and help me defend him. All of his friends that was in the church has called for their letters. Cobb and lady, and Mrs.Warden, old man and lady and Jim and Liddy Hardy, Harrison and old Ingrum won't go to church. They don't want to go back on brother Harben. If you want to hear any more come over one night next week and I will give the full details. John Rueben Rucher has had his trial. He was sentenced to the penitentiary for five years if he should live so long. I will close as Mollie wants to write some. Come soon and stay all night with me. Matt

Mrs. Ferguson

Dear friend,

I will try to write you a few lines. I suppose you think we was a long time, but you must excuse us, for we was waiting for some things to terminate. As Matt has given you all the news, I am at a loss what to write. We have fine gardens, vegetables a plenty. We have had any amount of rain this year. Everything looks splendid. We have a fine school. Miss Molly McLure is our teacher. Jimmie says tell Johnie [Margaret Jane's son] him and Alton is going to school. Tom will start soon. Tell Floyd [Margaret Jane's son] he must come over and go to school with Alton. Tell Nora [Margaret Jane's daughter] May is as fat as a pig and talks of her very often.

My baby can crawl. He is sick very near all the time from teething. Mrs. Ross come back from Austin all right except ill health. She is at work as same as ever. Miss Minnie Campbell I understand has swallowed a bean and it is sprouting, so her and old Harben is the topic of the day. Write soon. My love to all.

Your devoted friend,
Mary Mead

It is not clear what kind of trials Matt Mead was referring to in this letter. One was apparently a criminal trial as the man was sent to prison. The church trials referred to could have been hearings to remove members from the church. In the Baptist church, members had to be voted in, and they could also be voted out. Members who misbehaved or were deemed unfit to be associated with the church were discussed at hearings and the membership voted on whether they could stay members or not. If members left voluntarily from the church, they asked for a letter confirming that they were members in good standing to take to their new church. In this case the church members appeared to be rather divided over the situation with Mr. Harben. These divisions or splits among the congregation when they involved a large group of members were often the way new churches were begun. People were dissatisfied, asked for their letters, left, and joined a different church or started a new one. The following is an example of a church letter for Mr. Ingraham Hudson.

> We the Baptist Church of Christ at Ioni do certify that our beloved brother, Ingraham Hudson is a member in full fellowship with us and at his request is hereby granted a letter of dismission from us when joined to another church of the same faith and wisdom by order of the church in conference on Saturday before the 4th Sabbath in February, A.D. 1875.

> T.H. Stovall, Mod. R.A. Edwards, CC"[4]

In the late 1880s in Texas and even before, the church and the school were the center of the community's social life, so they were common subjects in family letters. Most of the Mead children were in school at this time, as were the Ferguson children who were approximately the same ages.

By 1880, Dan and Martha Huddleston were living in Wise County, Texas, in the Boonsville area. They had a sixth son in 1881, Reubin.[5] Also in 1881, Mary Elizabeth and Harmon Squyres in Hood County had another baby, a second daughter, Mary Etta.[6] In 1881, Lizzie wrote her sister at Alder Branch the following letter.

July 3
Dear sister,

It is with pleasure that I seat myself to write you a few lines. We are all well at present hoping these few lines may come safe to hand and find you all enjoying the same blessing. The health of this community is good so far as I know. I was sorry to hear you and the children had been sick. Jeff Guy [Caroline Jordan Guy's husband] has been disabled from work the most of this season with one of his eyes. He does not suffer with it now. He can't see but little out of it. We have had a very dry summer. We did not have any rain in June. The first day of July it rained all around. It rained hard at Granbury. We had a shower. Corn crops is cut short. We has very good corn considering the drouth. Some has none but has old corn enough to do them another year. Harmon thinks he will make enough to do him. Cotton looks very well. I did not make much garden. I made the finest onion I have made since we came out here. I have a great many chickens. I have thirteen little ducks and eleven eggs setting. I don't know of anything I could write that would interest you. I will quit for today. Well, Maggie, as I expect a chance to send this to the office tomorrow, I will finish it. My babe can sit alone. It can slide around all over the room. It is the best babe I ever saw as well as I can recollect. I often wish you could see Etta. I have pieced one quilt and put one together I haven't quilted any yet. Write soon and often. Your sister,

M.E. Squyres

Another letter from Lizzie to her sister Margaret Jane at Alder Branch in 1882 revealed more of life at Granbury in Hood County. The years spent at Granbury were the beginnings of stability for the Squyres and the Wyatt Jordan family. They moved around in the area, but not away from Hood County, and the Squyres even moved into town at one point. Not since the 1850s in Louisiana before the war had they stayed so long in one place. No one was getting rich, but no one was starving either. Life was moving on and becoming more settled which was a relief after the upheaval of the Civil War and its aftermath.

Granbury, Texas
January 29, 1882
Dear sister and family,

It is with pleasure that I seat myself this Sabbath evening to answer your very kind letter we received last evening. We was very glad to hear from you. The family is all well except myself. I have been sick a great deal lately with that old illness I used to have. I am under the treatment of a doctor. Well Mag, we are living in a house near the Granbury College. January the 30th Etta will be one year old today. She has been walking for four weeks. She does not try to talk yet. I can't stay but one week by myself since we moved. Sis stayed with me one week and cousin is staying with me now. Well Mag, there is a great deal of moving on Nubin Ridge this month. Simon [Wyatt Jordan's son] has moved to Autry. Andrew [Wyatt Jordan's son] has gone also. Guy Murphey is still living where he was when you left. Nate Roberson and Sudie Daniels is married. Miss Sinthey Po and Mr. Jones is married. I saw Ed Edens after the parson conducted the ceremony for Larro Edens yesterday. I did not learn the man's name. We have had quite a light winter. We had a light snow week before last. It snowed yesterday and sleeted last night. It is all melted now. I received a letter from sister Mat the same time I received yours. Everyone was all well and well satisfied. I heard from Pa and Ma and the boys about the same time. I would be glad to hear from you. You must write to me soon. Write whatever you have. I do not know any more that would interest you. I believe everyone has plenty to eat. I don't hear any complaints. Corn is worth one dollar per bushel, some meat is at 14 cents dried, wheat is very fine. There has been a great deal of wheat. I have forgotten what you have written. Do not wait so long to write.

M.E. Squyres
Freddy and Emma is going to school.

While the Squyres and Jordans were in Hood Co. in 1880, the Huddlestons were in Wise Co. establishing their farming/ranching business and raising a family. The senior Jordans, William and Martha were in Navarro County with their sons Perry and William and their families.[7] Perry and Mary Ann had arrived in Navarro County just before 1880, and in 1880 their third son arrived, James Luther.[8] In March of 1881 William C. and Francis had a daughter, Lula Ella.[9] However, in November of 1881, tragedy struck the family.[10] Francis died, and thus began a strange sequence of events - another mystery in the Jordan family. After Francis died, the Jordans decided to move out to Wise Co. where Dan and Martha Huddleston were living. They apparently had become unhappy with Navarro County, perhaps because of the mud, and Francis's death was the final impetus for the move. They went to the Garvin area which was several miles east of where the Huddlestons were living near Boonsville.

Back row: Lillian Lena Jordan, Joseph C. Jordan, Pearl Haney.
Seated: Josephine Holden Haney Jordan

In 1883, William C. remarried. Josephine Haney was a widow with two daughters, and the combined family began living in the Cottondale area. William and Josephine had a son together, Adolphus, born in 1884.[11] The family mystery surrounds what happened to William's baby, Lula, after the marriage. There is no record of her until the mid 1890s when she is living with the Squyres. Years later Lula would say that she grew up in the Butler orphanage, but there was no such place. Where was she for those missing years, and why wasn't she with her father or some other family member? Perhaps some explanation could be found in the accounts of Josephine Holden Haney Jordan's descendants which pictured her as a mean-spirited woman who treated all of her children badly. This may or may not have been true, and if it was true, how did it affect what happened to Lula? Did Josephine refuse to care for this baby and give the baby to another couple to raise? The events surrounding Lula's early life remain shrouded in mystery.[12]

Southern Wise County around Garvin and Boonsville was rolling hill country with a great many trees and some brush to border the wide open fields. It was mostly pastureland, but the brownish red soil would grow crops as well. The county seat was Decatur, not too far from Dallas and Ft. Worth. It was similar country to Navarro and Hood Counties with healthy, dry air and fewer insects.[13] The elder Jordans and Perry and his family were content with Wise County. They stayed and built farms, and Perry and Mary Ann raised a large family. After being apart for a number of years, the elder Jordans and Perry's family enjoyed being close to Martha and Dan Huddleston and their children.

On the other hand, William C. and Josephine stayed only until around 1887 and then moved on about 80 miles northwest in Texas to Wilbarger County.[14] Wilbarger County, Texas, and the Vernon area especially, was wide open range country and contained the Great Western Trail which cattle drives from the southernmost part of Texas all the way to the Red River had used since 1874. After crossing the Red River at Doan's Crossing, the trail continued as far north as South Dakota with trail head stops in Kansas and Nebraska for shipping the cattle back East. The cattle drives came to a close in the 1890s, but Wilbarger Co. continued to represent the real West which cowboy stories and dime novels had made famous. Not too many years before the Jordans arrived in the county, the area had been experiencing trouble with Indian uprisings.[15] William C. Jordan and his family bought land not too far from Vernon, Texas.[16] It is not known whether William tried raising cattle himself or just worked for neighboring ranches.

The Huddlestons had three more sons in this time period, Joseph Price in 1885, Pleasant "Jim" in 1886, and Henry in 1888.[17] Perry and Molly had three girls, Minnie Juel in 1882, Martha Cordelia in 1884, and Maude Carrie in 1886.[18] At Alder Branch, the Fergusons had another son, William Hugh in 1883.[19] This was their last child, and even though they had moved to different areas of Texas at various times, all of their children had been born at Alder Branch and two were likely buried there.

By 1888, all of the younger children of Wyatt Jordan were married and having children of their own. Simeon Jordan, named for his father's brother in Mississippi, married M.L. Rodgers on August 31, 1879. Emily Jordan married J.W. Leese or perhaps

Lusk on January 24, 1886. Tabitha Jordan married John Windom on January 13, 1882, and Andrew Jordan, the last to marry, married Mrs. M.A. Edens on September 16, 1888.[20] There is no mention of Isaac Jordan or Wilson Jordan after the 1870 census in Henderson County, Texas, so they must have lived apart from the rest of the family or died young. The two older girls in Wyatt Jordan's family who had been married in Louisiana, Caroline and Julia Ann, continued to have children and eventually moved on to other counties in Texas. Caroline Guy moved from Hood to Polk to Somervell County and finally to Kaufman County where she stayed until her death in 1904. Her husband William remarried twice, died in 1924, and is buried with her in Kaufman County at the Spikes Cemetery. Julia Ann Murphey moved from Hood County to Frankston, Texas in Anderson County where she lived out her life with her husband John. Julia died in 1929. Many of her descendants are buried with her at Frankston.[21]

The 1880s were good years for the most part for the Jordan families, a time to establish homes and raise the next generation. The families were growing larger, and the older grandchildren were growing up. Health concerns were ever present and bad crop years were always a possibility, but life was more peaceful because the Jordans had been able to establish a normal routine – at least until someone got the itch to move on to a better place.

Coppras Cove Coryell Texas 4c 21"
                My Dear friend I D Ferguson
I Will now try to fullfill my Promis
Wee landed here all Write Pa has rented a plase
it is good land to the best I ever saw I think
Wee Con make a living if We half try Mastood
the trip very Well but she has a terbel cold they
Was too days Coming from & Palestine here
I Went to Church onst ther I Was at Cary's
I Seen your a girl at Church she is as prty as ever
but not as prty as the Coryell girls girls
it Would make your Mouth Walles to See some of them
I like this Cuntry very Well Wee are living on the
Prairie you I Con get out and See as far as I Want
to no Brush to Bother me all I Want is
Some gay hounds to run mule rabits you must
not expect a long letter letter for I have no news
To Write but I Want you to Write me a long letter
Sent Durect to Coppras Cove Coryell Texas
                I As ever your friend
                    Robert Hudson

R. H. HILL, Principal and Proprietor.
F. M. ALLEN, Vice-Principal.

—OFFICE OF—

FOUNDED IN 1881.
CHARTERED IN 1882.

Hill's Practical Business College

The Largest Business College in the Southern States,
All Departments Complete and Comprehensive

Waco, Tex. Feb. 2, 1885

Mr. John Ferguson,
Elder Branch, Tex.

Dear friend,

Your letter has been received, consumed, and digested. It was so long before I received it I thought you had forgotten to write to me. My health is pretty good now but I had a pretty hard time last week, I had what they call slow fever. Was surprised to hear of those boys getting off to school. Will M. was talking of going off where I left but I didn't think he had much intention of going. I'm getting along very well

with my studies now, I'm
on examination for the practical now, don't know
whether I'll get through or
not but you bet I'll bother
them considerably if I don't
Was glad to hear you had
such nice dances there it
nearly makes me homesick
to think of it I wish I had
been there. I hope Miss Ida
is stuck on me, nothing
could please me better, you
mustn't set her too heavy.
Tell all the girls I love 'em
and write soon.
Kind love to all, Yours truly
N. Burke

Chapter 19

From 1883 to 1885 friends and relatives wrote a number of letters to John D. (Johnny) Ferguson, son of Margaret Jane and John T. Ferguson, who was around sixteen years old at the time. These letters revealed what it was like to be a young person in the 1880s American West with whole new worlds to conquer, where anything was possible once again, and no war was on the horizon. The sons and daughters of the people who had survived the Civil War and its aftermath had been touched by the tragedy of war as it affected their parents, but because of their youth, they carried a new optimistic spirit into the decades which followed and which would be theirs to mold. A new generation was getting ready to try its hand at making a living and building a life. The following letter is an example of the plans and preoccupations of youth in the 1880s.

Omen Smith Co., Texas
February 23, 1883
Mr. John Ferguson Jr.
Dear friend,
    I am here and am going to school and am getting along very well. I am well pleased with this school. We have good teachers here. There is about seventy or eighty students in school. There is twenty-six students in my Algebra class and the same in my arithmetic. We have a reading club every Friday night and debate on Saturday night. I went to church last Sabbath and to Sabbath school in the evening. Well John, there is some pretty girls here, but we are not allowed to go with them but once a month.
    I am well pleased with this country. Although there has been some very cold weather since we have been here, there has been two snows, and it is raining now. Well John, I want you to tell me about the girls, and I don't want you to get ahead of me while I am gone. I want you to tell me about Miss Ida, and don't you set

to her too much, boy.

Well, I have nothing to write of much interest. Will and I have got a good boarding place. We have to pay ten dollars per month for board and washing. My tuition is three and a half dollars per month. There is four others boarding at the same place. We have to study till ten o'clock at night. The boys are all busy now, and I am getting tired. I have not heard from home since I left. So nothing more at present. Write to me soon. Wishing you good luck, I remain your friend. Give my regards to all and accept the same.

George Scarbrough

Going away from home for schooling was necessary in the 1880s, especially for secondary or high school. Community elementary or primary school ended with the 8th grade, and this was all the education that most people had, if they had that much. In the second decade after the Civil War, families in the West felt in increasing numbers that it was important to have a higher education in order to get ahead, to be successful, and to compete with people raised in the East. Thus more schools came into being to provide this higher education.[1] Some schools undoubtedly had their own boarding facilities, but others asked their students to find room and board in the town where the school was located. This was the case with George Scarbrough. The schools were pretty strictly run which accounted for the crimp in George's social life and his extensive study hours. The cost of his education, although minimal when compared to late twentieth century standards, was probably sizable when compared to his parents' income. Albert Burke was another friend of Johnny's away at school.

Hill's Practical Business College
Waco, Texas
January 29, 1885
Mr. J.D. Ferguson [John Jr.]
Alder Branch, Texas
Esteemed friend,

Well, I am here and am going to school. I think it's a fine

school. Never thought there was so much to learn about bookkeeping before. I tell you it's naturally hard to learn. They all say I'm getting along very fast for a fellow that never studied bookkeeping. I'll get through in about four months. Have had the worst weather you ever saw since I got here. John, I can't write any more tonight. Write soon. As ever yours truly. Albert

February 21, 1885
Alder Branch, Texas
Mr. John Ferguson [John Jr.]
Dear friend,
    Your letter has been received, consumed, and digested. It was so long before I received it I thought you had forgotten to write to me. My health is pretty good now but I had a pretty hard twist last week. I had what they call slow fever. Was surprised to hear of those boys getting off to school. Will M. was talking of going off when I left but I didn't think he had much intention of going. I'm getting along very well with my studies now. I'm on examination for the practical now. Don't know whether I'll get through or not, but you bet I'll bother them considerably if I don't. Was glad to hear you had such nice dances there. It nearly makes me homesick to think of it. I wish I had been there. I hope Miss Ida is stuck on me. Nothing could please me better. You mustn't set her too heavy. Tell all the girls I love'em and write soon. Send love to all.

Yours truly,
Burke

    Albert's letters certainly reflected his chosen field of study at school. His voice was very business-like and professional, that is, until he asked about the neighborhood girls. Then he slid back into the vernacular of all the young men of his acquaintance and their pressing preoccupation with the opposite sex. It is interesting to note that two of John's friends asked about Miss Ida in their letters. She must have been the most popular girl in the neighborhood. Albert also wrote about being sick with fever. Even tough, young men at boarding school were not exempt from illness in the 1880s. The length of Albert's course of study was four months to qualify him for a career in bookkeeping. Most of the disciplines taught in higher education required only relatively short lengths of study to qualify people for careers. Some careers required apprenticeships as well as education, but in general, the public still thought experience was the best teacher, and education was not necessarily a lengthy process. A university education was possible but mostly for the wealthy. Universities in the West were just coming into being and were small colleges at best. The larger, more prestigious universities were all in the East and fairly inaccessible unless the parents had some connections and money.[2] However, as evidenced by the following letter, not every young man was attending school in the 1880s.

September 7, 1884
Van Zandt County
John Ferguson Jr.
Dear sir:

   I seat myself to drop you a few lines to let you know that I am well, hoping when these few lines comes to hand, they will find you enjoying the same. I am in Van Zandt County working for a man by the name of Herrin for $100 per month. I want you to write me the news generally, especially about my girl. Also write to me how Mr. Middleton is getting along gathering my crop. Please write me soon as you get this. Yours as ever.

W.H. Turner
Direct your letters to Henderson County, Goshen Post Office, Texas.

   This friend of Johnny's was working instead of going to school, but he had the same concerns about being away from home. Was he missing out on anything? How was his girlfriend? Was the person taking care of his property doing a good job? Coincidentally, these were the same concerns of the young men of a generation before, far from home fighting in a war they felt was necessary to win to ensure their future. Many things changed with the Civil War, but some things stayed the same.

   Some of Johnny's friends moved further west with their families, and this presented a chance for adventure and the promise of a better place with more opportunity. A new beginning on virgin land was a challenge that excited young and old alike. As people moved westward in Texas, they discovered the endless prairies of the real West. For some, the open country was frightening and too barren. For others, it represented the freedom of unlimited choices, no barriers, a land wild and untamed but rich with promise. It especially appealed to the young.

Copperas Cove, Texas
Coryell County
December 21, 1884
J.D. Ferguson [John Jr.]
My dear friend,

I will now try to fulfill my promise. We landed here all right. Pa has rented a place. It is good land too - the best I ever saw. I think we can make a living if we half try. Ma stood the trip very well, but she has a fearful cold. They was two days coming from Palestine here. I went to church, and when I was at Cory's, I seen your girl at church. She is as pretty as ever but not as pretty as the Coryell girls. It would make your mouth water to see some of them. I like this country very well. We are living on the prairie. I can get out and see as far as I want to, no brush to bother me. All I want is some greyhounds to run mule rabbits. You must not expect a long letter for I have no news to write, but I want you to write me a long letter. Direct to Copperas Cove, Coryell Co., Texas.

As ever your friend,
Robert Hudson

Copperas Cove, Texas
August 15, 1885
Mr. Ferguson [John Jr.]
My dear old friend,

After a long time I will write to you again. Don't think that I have forgotten you. Well, I don't know much to write, but I thought I would write to you to show you that I hadn't forgotten you. Well, I like this country fine if I could get some of you boys out here with me. I have been going to school for some time. The school is out, and I have to go to pick cotton, and you know that will go mighty hard with me. I was at a picnic on the 10th. It was on the Cowhouse [creek which ran through Coryell County]. We had a fine time - had plenty of fish.

Well, you must excuse the letter for it was written in a hurry. Ma said tell your ma that she certainly had forgot her. I will close. I want you to write to me soon and write me a letter as long as your arm. Well, I will close with best respects to you all.

R.L. Hudson

Tom Mead was another friend to write from a new location in Texas where his family had moved. He was the son of Matt and Mary Mead, friends of Johnny Ferguson's father and mother.

McGregor, Texas
June 22, 1885
Dear friend,

I will endeavor to write you a few lines in answer to yours after so long a time. Well John, I have no news to tell you. We are all enjoying good health. Pa is in better health than he has been in two or three years. Well John, I have not been sick a day since I came out here.

We have got our cotton plowed out once and hoed twice. We are all needing rain. Aunt Sarah Morrison is very low. She has congestion of the lungs. I reckon we will start to school next week. I want to go very bad. John, you ought to be out here to see some of the country, not stay back there in the woods. I want to know when you are coming to me. This leaves all well. Write soon and often to your friend.

T.E. Mead

Note to Mr. Ferguson on back:

Well, Mr. Ferguson, I will write you a few lines. I want you to tell me how Grandpa and Grandma is getting along. Well Mr. Ferguson, we have a very pretty prospect for a crop. Well, I will have to close. Give my love to all the children. Write soon and often to your friend.

T.E. Mead

McGregor, Texas
McLennan Co.
August 28, 1885
Mr. Johnnie Ferguson
Dear old school mate,

I will endeavor to answer your kind and welcome letter I received some time since. John, I would like to see you just now. I reckon we will come back to old Anderson [County] this winter. John, I would have written sooner, but I nearly forgot to write, but I will make up for last time. John, I heard that Ross killed Henry Thornton, and if I heard it straight, he was justified. John, I have no more news to write you. Well, there is no sickness here that I know of (but I don't know anybody hardly) here.

Well, I reckon I had better quit for this time, but I want to know something about how your crop is looking. Tell Mr. Ferguson to write. I haven't time for I have to go to the post office this evening. John, write to me and tell me all the news you know of in the country. Well, give my love to all and share a large portion for yourself. This leaves all well. Write soon and often. Your friend,

Tom Mead Esq.

Back side of letter has math rules at the top and this note:
John, excuse this for I wrote on this before I noticed it, but it is nothing but a rule which is very common in arithmetic. I haven't time to write another. Tom

It is not known whether the Mead family was moving back to Anderson County in the winter or just visiting. They were living at McGregor, Texas, when Tom wrote his letters, and five years previously they had been at Ioni, Texas, when they wrote to John and Margaret Ferguson. When people moved away, they sometimes returned to the home place when they didn't prosper. This was the case with the Ferguson family who had moved back and forth several times. Anderson County was familiar territory for them, if not always the healthiest place to be living. Also in August of 1885, Johnny heard from his cousin, Emma Squyres, Harmon and Lizzie's daughter, now fifteen years old.

Granbury, Texas
August 16, 1885
Mr. John D. Ferguson [John Jr.]
Dear cousin,

It is with much pleasure I seat myself this beautiful Sabbath morning to answer your kind and intelligent letter which I received some time ago. Oh! How glad I was to get a letter from you, Johnie. It made me feel like I was not entirely forgotten by you. I wish you could be here today. Grandma is here and Grandpa [William and Martha Jordan] and Uncle Dan [Huddleston] came Thursday, and Friday they went to Cousin Jeff G. [Guy]. Yesterday they went to Cousin Simon J. [Jordan] and today they will come back, and cousin John Squyres of Cleburne will be here today - him and his wife.

Well Johnie, we have had a hard time since I written to you. I have been sick and Pa had a mighty bad spell. He lay twelve days that he never sat up any at all. I have had the sore eyes, and now I am crippled. I have got a sore foot. It has been sore a week yesterday. I can't wear a shoe yet. Oh, don't you know I get tired.

John, you did not tell me what you had done with Miss Albie nor what your girl's name is. How long is it going to be before you can send me your picture? Well, Johnie, I had forgotten to tell you of our misfortune. One of Pa's best horses died this last week. She was foundered on green corn. Oh! It was so bad on us, but I guess it was all for the best or the good Lord would not of taken her away. I feel this morning like if we will put our trust in Him, He will bless us. I must close. Write soon. We are all up this morning, and I hope this will find you all well.

Emma Squyres

This letter recounted some of the trials and tribulations of the Squyres family of which there always seemed to be plenty. However, it also illustrated the abiding faith in God that the entire Jordan family shared and which helped them to endure and find their own measure of peace. This was a continuing theme through all the voices in the family letters. Their faith in a higher wisdom was all that they had to cling to at times, that and their sense of humor and their belief in themselves. The letter also mentioned other family members visiting the Squyres on that Sunday in 1885. The elder Jordans and the Huddlestons in Wise County lived fairly close to the Squyres and were apparently able to visit them and the Wyatt Jordan offspring in Hood County on occasion. The Fergusons were the farthest away from the family at this time, living at Alder Branch. Undoubtedly, part of the reason Emma was optimistic on that Sunday morning was because so many of her family were visiting. Other than faith in God, family was the most important thing in the Jordans' lives, giving them riches beyond money and possessions.

As illustrated in these letters, Johnny Ferguson and his friends were doing what their parents had done before them, preparing themselves to earn a living and going out to wrest from life the best that it had to offer. They hoped that the country would pull itself together, and they would have a more prosperous life than their parents. Unlike their parents, they weren't all going to become farmers and ranchers because in the 1880s there were more choices available to young people, especially those who had an education. With the approach of the new century, there was hope that people would find success once again and be able to finally shake off the harsh Civil War and Reconstruction years. The next generation was ready to start building the future.

Chapter 20

The mail in the mid to late 1880s could still be erratic, but it also continued to be a great source of entertainment and information for the people of Texas at that time. Newspapers were available in the larger cities, but they rarely contained any personal family news. Small town newspapers sometimes carried tidbits of news about the local citizenry, but the personal letter was the only way to hear the voice of a loved one. During this time period, not only was William Jordan getting letters from his children but he was starting to hear from his grandchildren as well.

Cleburne, Texas
September 22, 1885
Mr. W.H. Jordan
Dear Grandfather and Grandmother,

I will write you a few lines this eve in answer to the one I received from you a few days ago. This leaves us all well and hope it will find you both in the best of health. I hardly know what to write that would interest you as news is very scarce in this section of the country. It has been quite awhile since we had a rain. Gardens have all dried up. The farmers are all busy in this section of the country picking cotton. Cotton is not turning out as well as most of people thought it would but it is selling for more this year than it did last. It has went as high as $1.75 in Cleburne, but I have heard that it has went to $2.50 in other places. Corn is very good. Small grain was not much and it was so wet at thrashing time that it did not save very well. I received a card from Ma the other day and they were all well [in Hood County]. I will close for this time. Hope to hear from you soon. I am respectfully

W.F. Squyres [William Fletcher Squyres]

William Fletcher Squyres, Harmon and Lizzie Squyres's son, was eighteen and living on his own at Cleburne, Texas, when he wrote this letter to his grandparents. His education was apparent in the letter; he had learned to write correctly and very well. He figured the only topic of conversation that would interest his grandpa and grandma was farming, so he wrote about the various crops and prices for those crops in his area. Often, letter writers included with their family news current prices for various livestock and crops as well as prices on bought goods at the store. Another popular topic for letters was the weather. Everyone had an opinion about it, and farmers especially liked to complain about it.

In December of 1884, John T. Ferguson received a letter at Alder Branch from a friend living in western Texas concerning various business arrangements. With so many people changing locations so frequently, keeping a steady cash flow coming in and supervising land transactions was difficult. Often people moved to a new place without selling the old one, thereby creating havoc with the tax rolls and land office records. It was commonplace to have friends or trusted acquaintances take care of business matters in the absence of the land or property owner. With the coming of the twentieth century, such trust and the need for it became less than commonplace.

Love Grove, Texas
December 18, 1884
J.T. Ferguson
Dear John,

I received your card and was glad to hear that you were all well. Hope this will find you all well. In relation to the business I will say that I can't help Mr. Jones or anyone else. Neither can I divide with Mr. Campbell or anyone else. I am building a house at Pontotoc, Mason County, and I will need every dollar that is due me and more too. Please ask those that are owing me there to help me a little every time you see them.

You had as well close out with Mr. Jones if he can't make any arrangements to furnish himself and rent the place if you can to someone who can furnish himself. Mr. Jones nor Mr.

Campbell have neither of them written to me on the subject and it would have done no good if they had.

John, I am satisfied that you will attend to my business as well or better than I would if I was there myself. The health of the country is very good. Fannie has been sick but is better. All the Anderson Co. folks that live here are well except Mr. Dunk's folks - they have the measles.

I want you to use your own judgement about selling that cotton, corn, and horses, and whatever money you have for me, hand it over to Mr. Royall. He sends it to me without any expense. Give our best respects to your family and all inquiring friends. I remain as ever

D.M. Anderson

P.S. Curtis is up at Pontotoc working on our house. He has got the measles but is better now. We will move about the first of next month. DMA

Anderson was building a new house in the Pontotoc area which was farther west in Texas, but he obviously still had business in Anderson County. He was relying on John Ferguson to handle some property for him and the sale of some crops. Another letter that John Ferguson received from a lawyer in 1885 illustrated again people's difficulties with land transactions. After John had bought land, he discovered through this letter that a lawyer held a claim on that land because of the former owner's failure to pay off his loan. This type of legal tangle was common in the 1880s when landowners were prone to move and not properly dispose of their property and debts.

R.A. Reeves, Attorney at Law
Palestine, Texas
October 1, 1885
Mr. John Ferguson
Alder Branch
Dear Sir:

I am informed that you bought Mr. Hudson's place being the place where you now reside. I write to inquire whether Mr. Hudson made any arrangement with you to pay off my claim on the land. I hold the notes for the purchase money which are liens on the land. Please let me hear from you. I must take steps to close out my claim unless satisfactorily arranged.

Yours respectfully,
R.A. Reeves

In 1887, John received another letter from D.M. Anderson revealing that the Andersons did in fact move to Pontotoc, Texas, and were doing well there. However, Anderson was still looking to collect the money owed him back in 1884. He spoke of the railroad coming to his county and of the people's doubts about it. The railroad companies were far from perfect in their business practices, mostly due to the tremendous profits at stake. However, in spite of the public's doubts and fears, slowly but surely, the railroads were spreading across America's western lands and bringing with them civilization and prosperity. Towns that were located on the railroads' route typically boomed. Towns which were not, struggled, and some died completely. The manufacturers and factories of the East were connected to the raw materials of the West, resulting in a better economy in both areas and wealth for the railroads. People had an easier way to travel and to move to new locations; therefore, the population of the West was growing. As a result, the Native Americans had no choice but to give ground to the white man and the "iron horse." The vast untamed West would never be the same again. However, travel, the mail delivery, and the movement of goods would get better and be more reliable. The abuses of the railroad companies were eventually curbed by some private intervention and also state and federal controls with the coming of the new century.[1]

Pontotoc, Texas
October 17, 1887
Mr. J.T. Ferguson
Friend John,

It has been a long time since I had a letter from you. I am certain I did not get an answer to my last one. We are all well. Mollie has had a spell of sickness lately but is now out of danger. We got a note from her yesterday and she had been to church.

Fannie's baby has been sick but is better. The balance of our connection is all well.

Billie has gone to Nashville again to attend the Vanderbuilt Medical College. They started last week. We have had an abundance of rain lately but it came too late to make good crops for us. Still we were glad to see it. We are expecting to have railroads and ironworks in Llano and also through this county in the near future. We don't know whether it will be for the best or not.

Old Dr. Reuben has bought a drove of horses and is going to take them to Georgia to sell next month. What is my prospect for getting money back there this fall? George Carroll wrote to Curtis that he would pay me this fall. I have heard that crops are very good, and it makes me hopeful of getting money. Will Mr. James Taylor pay what he owes me soon?

Our school is in good condition and well attended. Give our best respects to your family and inquiring friends.

Your friend and brother,
D.M. Anderson

The people of Texas were still connected to the South in many ways. They sometimes were able to send their children back to the South to attend college at established universities. They also created opportunities for commerce with Southern merchants by collecting certain desired raw materials such as horses or cattle and delivering them for sale to these merchants. During these years, survival depended upon being creative and willing to try new things. People in one occupation would try something else as well to try to bring in more money. Survival also depended upon maintaining old loyalties and cultivating new ones. Prosperity could as easily come from an old association as from a new venture.

The last surviving Jordan letter of the 1880s was written by William H. Jordan to Margaret Jane and John at Alder Branch in 1887. It contained not only family news but some commentary on the concerns of the times. In many ways it was a summation of the family's journey through Reconstruction and its struggle to survive using any means possible.

Garvin
July the 28, 1887
Dear Mag and John,

I will write you a few lines to let you know that I and Ma is both well. Hope these lines will come safe to hand and find you all well. We had a fine rain the fourth of July but the hot wind and dry weather burnt up our corn. Some say they will not make as much corn as they made last year. Some has good corn. Cotton was the finest two weeks ago that I ever saw at this season but cotton is nearly all shed off but the people say it is time enough to make a good crop of cotton if it rains shortly and no disaster [like] the worm is in the cotton.

Big meetings is now running. Jest closed a camp meeting at Garvin, lasted eight days. They had a big time. They have considerable revivals at all the meetings I have heard from, protracted meetings. Dan has a sorry crop, haven't had but little rain. William is in Wilbarger County. They are burnt up there. He is in the stock business. He writes they have fine grass. His address is Talmedge, Wilbarger County. Perry is now in Ft. Worth selling albums. I am selling Bibles. I am thinking of taking the agency for several other works if it will rain shortly. I wrote you last fall to know if there were many book agents in that country and how books would sell there but you never answered it. I had thought of coming there to canvass with books. I followed that business some last summer and fall. I have applications now from different firms to canvass with different books. I have been traveling some with the Bible. The prospect is at present too gloomy to sell books here now.

Well, the election is near at hand, and I never have seen in all my life so great excitement about an election that have been for weeks the conversation of the day at church, at home and abroad. I have heard of a goodly number being killed over the Prohibition question. Well I do not bother myself with it and I don't bother anyone else. Yes, they can't find out how I am going to vote and that bothers them to some extent. I want to hear how the times is in Anderson. Write something uncle buck.

W.H. Jordan

In 1887, there was a political campaign to pass a prohibition amendment to the Texas constitution outlawing the sale of alcohol. Although the amendment was eventually defeated in 1887, the issue continued to be fiercely debated.[2] Apparently William was keeping his own council on the Prohibition question. That was probably the safest position to take because as he noted, the issue provoked violent reactions from people. There was no sense in getting killed over it, especially if he had no strong opinion either way. He also seemed to enjoy keeping people guessing. Texas was still a fairly violent place in the late 1880s. It had always been rough and wild with outlaws and men of a volatile nature, and that reputation lingered on as the century drew to a close. As evidence of this, several incidents of murders and killings were recalled in the Jordan family letters by friends as well as family members. However, what was not recounted in the Jordan letters was trouble with Native Americans. Although the family lived on the edge of the frontier at times, most of the Indian fighting was over by the time the family arrived on the scene.

Religion and church life were accepted facts for most people, partially because they, along with education, were a civilizing influence on towns. With some religions this included camp meetings or revivals. These were special meetings of church people at special locations, sometimes in large tents, to encourage other members of the community to become Christians and join the church sponsoring the meeting. The meetings also served to increase the commitment of the people who were already members of the church. Usually a speaker, often fervent, other than the local church minister was asked to come and preach the sermons. Some of these speakers traveled around the country and preached at these meetings for a living, so they were not always invited by the local church but found support there for their meetings when they arrived in town. Family correspondence often referred to attending one of these gatherings.[3] For years, they had been common among Baptist congregations across the South and West. More than religion was involved, as people used these meetings for getting together with neighbors and socializing.

Even with William's strong interest in religion, he probably never in his wildest dreams as a boy growing up on a Mississippi plantation would have pictured himself as a Bible salesman, but the man he became would not turn away from an opportunity to make a few extra dollars. He was a survivor and enterprising enough to try anything. Some of the rest of the family, at least occasionally, tried other occupations besides their normal agricultural pursuits. Like his father, Perry worked at selling. In 1887, he was selling albums in Ft. Worth. He had been a minister in Cherokee County in the 1870s, and at a later time he tried inventing new farm equipment. John, Margaret's husband, worked as an itinerant minister. Harmon Squyres, Mary Elizabeth's husband, did carpentry work when he could find it. The family as a whole managed to survive the Reconstruction years, working at a little bit of this and a little bit of that and staying away from politics and dangerous situations. They had each other, their church life, and work on the land that seemed ever-present in their lives. It was enough.

In 1889 William C. Jordan in Wilbarger County, Texas, and his wife Josie had a daughter Lillian Lena. This was their last child, giving them two children together, two by William's first marriage and two by Josie's first marriage. Unfortunately also in 1889, Johnny Ferguson, Margaret Jane and John's son, died unexpectedly at the young age of twenty-one from yellow jaundice. In modern medical terms, the jaundice could have been liver disease or a symptom of malaria or hepatitis rather than a disease in itself, but it would have been difficult to treat without the antibiotics of the twentieth century. In Johnny's memory, his mother saved the letters that his friends had written to him, testimonials of bright hopes that would never be realized in Johnny's case. Margaret Jane had four children left, and her own health was not good. Maybe it was time to think of moving to a new, healthier location. With the coming of the 1890s, W. H. Jordan's mind was also on moving, indicating his long stay in Wise County was coming to an end. Those itchy feet were calling again, and it was time for Martha to pack up the dishes and get ready to go.

Cleburne Texas
September 22, 1895
Mr. Wm H. Jordan,
Dear Grand Father &
Grand Mother I will write
you a few lines, this
eve, in answer to the one
I received from you a few
days ago this leaves
us all well and hope
it will find you Both in
the Best of health,
I hardley Know what
to writ that would
interest you as news
is very scarce in this
section of the country
it has ben quite a while
serve we had a rain
gardains have all died
up, the Farmers are all

Buisey in this section
of the country ppicking
cotton, cotton is not
turning out as well as
most of people thought
it would but it is
~~selling for more this year~~
than it did last. it has
went as high 7⁷⁵ in
Cleburne but I have heard
that it has went to 8⁵⁰
in other places. corn is
very good small grain
was not ~~nintch~~ and it
was so well at thrashing
~~time that it did not last~~
very well. I received
a card from ma the other
day and they were all well.
I will close for this
time hope to hear from
you soon I am R~~espectfully~~
Respectifully W, F, Squyres
Cleburne

Garvin July the 28 1887

Dear Mrg & John

I will wright you afiew lines to let you
no that I & Ma is both well, hope those
lines will come ~~safe~~ to hand and find you
all well, we had afine rain the forth of July
but the hot wind and dry weather burnt up
our Corn some say they will not make
as much Corn as they made last year
some has good Corn Cotto was the finest
two weaks ago that I ever saw at this season but Cotton
is ~~poor~~ and ~~well of~~ but the people say
it is time enough to make a glad Crop
of Cotton - if it Rains shortly and no ~~drouth~~
the worm is in the Cotton, Big meatings is
now ganning just closed a campmeeting at
Garvin lested 8 days they had abig time they
~~had another~~ ~~~~
~~hear from~~ Protracted Meetings, Dan has a ~~very~~
Crop havent had but little rain, William is
in Wilbarger County they are burnt up there
he is in the stock buisness he wright they have
fine grass hisaddress is Talmedge Wilbarger co
Perry is now in Fortworth selling Albums

I am selling Bibles. I am thinking of taking
the agency for several other works if it will
pain Mostly I wrote you last fall to no if
there were many Book agents in that country and how Books sold field there but
you never answered it I had thought of
comeing there to Canvass with Books,
I followed that buisnes some last summer and
fall, I have applications now from diferent firms
to canvass with diferent Books I have bin
travlen some with the Bible, the prospect is
at preasant to gloomy to sell Books hear now
Well the Election is near at hand and I never
have seen in all my life so great excitement
about an election that have bin for weaks
the converstion of the day at Church at home
and abroad I have heard of a goodly number being
held over the Prosecution question well I do not
bother my selfe with it and I dont bother any one
else yet they cant find out how I am going to
vote and that bothers them to some extent
I want to hear how the times is in Anderson weigh
at some thing uncle Buck,

                    W. H. Jordan

Chapter 21

The 1890s in Texas found the Jordan family and its extended branches occupied with the same pursuits but in different locations. William and Martha moved from the Garvin area of Wise County, Texas, to Percilla in Houston County around 1893. They had come almost full circle from when they first arrived in Texas in 1863, being only a few miles from Anderson County and Palestine, Texas. After thirty years, they were right back where they started in more ways than one. Their economic condition consisted of owning no property and earning just enough to keep food on the table and a roof over their heads. By 1893 William was no longer farming or ranching because he was 76 years old. Perhaps in their last years William and Martha wanted to live close to Margaret Jane and John Ferguson, and the Fergusons had moved to the Percilla area around 1891. The Jordans probably rented a small place in or near Percilla, Texas, and Margaret and John were there to help when needed.[1]

The decade began on a sad note with the death of another of William and Martha's children. William C. Jordan died in January of 1890 in Wilbarger County, Texas, at the age of thirty-five.[2] He was William and Martha's youngest child, and like so many of their children, he died young or at least comparatively so. His cause of death is not known, nor is his place of burial. Shortly before his death, he and his wife sold the land on which they had been ranching and perhaps moved into or closer to Vernon, Texas.[3] His family life after his second marriage had been clouded apparently, and then the five children, the oldest being twelve, were left for his wife to raise, sometimes in neglect, after his untimely death. However, most of the children managed to grow up and become independent in spite of their bumpy childhood. Of the two children that William and Josie had together, the youngest, Lena, married William Thomas Miller in 1906 and raised a large family. Unfortunately, Lena's older brother Adolphus died young at the age of fourteen in 1898. Josephine Jordan continued to buy and sell land for awhile in Wilbarger Co. in the years that followed, and she moved back and forth to Wise County. She lived out her last years in Wise County and died in 1938.[4] She, her daughter Pearl by her first marriage, and Pearl's two daughters are buried at Cottondale Cemetery near Paradise, Texas.[5] With the death of William C., only four of William and Martha Jordan's children remained to outlive them, a circumstance that no parent would welcome.

However, the Jordans had many grandchildren. Another Jordan grandchild was born to Dan and Martha Huddleston in 1890, a son named Matthew E. The Huddlestons also lost a child the next year in 1891, their son, Henry C. who was around three years old. In 1892 a daughter, Lillian, was born to them. Lillian was Dan and Martha's first daughter after having ten sons. What a cause for celebration! Lillian grew up to become a high school teacher at Bridgeport in Wise County, Texas, and took care of her parents until they died. She waited to marry until after their deaths. The Huddlestons had two more children, Myra in 1895 who only lived a month, and Ferman G. in 1896.[6] In1892 another son, John Perry, was born to Perry and Mary Ann, and in 1894, their last child was born, a son named Charles Franklin.[7] The descendants of Charles Franklin, or Frank as he was known, recall that he and Perry did not have a good relationship. For some reason, Perry abused his last child until Frank ran away from home at the age of fourteen, stealing a saddle and a rifle and joining a cattle drive. He worked the cattle drives until he married and settled down in New Mexico. In later years he was in contact with his family and lived close to them at times, so his running away at fourteen was not a permanent estrangement from the family. He and his sons were in the shoe repair, leather products, and saddle making business as well as farming and ranching. Some of his sons also became ministers.[8]

By 1895, several of the oldest Jordan grandchildren were married and were starting families of their own, so a new generation of Jordans was beginning. These included Dan and Martha Huddleston's two oldest boys, Mary Elizabeth Squyres oldest son and daughter, and Margaret Jane and John Ferguson's son, Thomas Floyd.[9] Thomas Floyd eloped with Willie Mae Lively in 1895, creating a story for the local Crockett newspaper.

> August 2, 1895: Mr. Loyd Anderson rode up to the Christian Sunday School a few evenings ago, and taking Miss Willie Lively, daughter of Taylor Lively, behind him on his horse, rode off in a hurry towards Mr. Johnson's residence and in the lane nearby delivered her to Mr. Floyd Ferguson in a buggy to whom she was married on the spot by Rev. J.E. Howard, who was in waiting nearby and the happy couple went their way rejoicing.[10]

In 1894 William Jordan at Percilla, Texas, received the following letter from a grandson living at Garvin, Texas. He mentions watermelons and peaches. These must have been favorite foods of the Jordans because in every generation, someone mentioned in a letter eating them or missing eating them.

Garvin, Texas
August 14, 1894
Mr. W.H. Jordan and wife
Dear friend,

I seat myself to answer your most kind and welcome letter that I received some time ago. I was glad to hear from you and to hear that you was all well. These few lines leaves us all as common. Harriet has been sick but she is up again. Well, grandpa, you said you had written me two letters before this card and I haven't received but one letter and one card from you. I want you to excuse me for not answering your letter sooner. I thought I would get some money for you when I wrote, but I haven't collected a cent for you and hardly ever see Blakston. But I told Luther and Eder Swinford what you said, but they haven't paid it yet. They keep saying they will but that is all. Well, grandpa, corn crops is about like they was last year. Cotton is the finest I ever saw if the worms don't eat the cotton. People will make all they can gather. I have got 40 acres in cotton. Well, grandpa, I was glad to hear that you was well pleased with your new country. Sam Wisdom died the 4th of this month. He fell out of the wagon and broke his hip. He lay there over two months but finally died. They had five doctors with him first and last. Well, grandpa, you don't know how bad I missed you and grandma and want to see you both mighty bad. Well, grandma, you just ought to see little Gracy Alice. She can run all over the place and can talk so sweet. The other children all talked a heap about grandpa and grandma after you all left for a long time. I wish you was here to help us eat watermelons and peaches. We have got plenty of them. Well, as I haven't any news to write I must close by asking you to write as soon as you get this. I remain as ever yours until death grandpa and grandma Jordan.

E.S. Townsend

This grandson's last name was Townsend, and he has not been traced to any Jordan child as of yet. This could suggest that there may have been another child for William and Martha. However, Townsend could have married a Jordan grandchild. This is another family mystery.

The Squyres home in Alvin, Texas
L to R: Harmon, Lizzie, and Etta

Around 1894, Harmon and Mary Elizabeth (Lizzie) Squyres moved to Alvin, Texas.[11] They were the first Jordan family members to move that far south in Texas - below Houston and close to the Gulf of Mexico. They were quite a distance from any of their family, but by that time it would have been easy to travel by train. However, it is doubtful that the Squyres had any money for traveling. Before they left Granbury and Hood County, their son, William Fletcher, married Maggie Iola Marlow on September 16, 1888, and their oldest daughter, Margaret Emma, married Frank A. McKinney on February 11, 1886.[12] Frank and Emma moved to the Alvin area with the Squyres as did William Fletcher and his wife.[13]

The William Jordans received the following letter from their grandaughter, Etta Squyres, Lizzie's youngest daughter, and her mother in 1895. Etta would have been thirteen years old.

Alvin, Texas
September 19, 1895
W.H. Jordan Percilla, Texas
Houston County
Dear Grandpa and Grandma,
   I will try and write you a few lines to let you know I am getting along all right going to school. I am in the eighth grade. School begun Monday morning. There was something over two hundred children begun school and there is several more going to start Monday morning.
   Well I have a nice time this summer going to parties. I haven't been to a party in about two or three weeks. The last one I went to was about three miles and a half from town. Mr. Cox taken Miss Iva McCreery and myself - had a nice time of course. Miss Iva is a very dear friend of mine. We are together so much. Last Sunday as a week, she came home with me from church and taken dinner with me in the afternoon. She and myself went out to Miss Kattie and Fannie Allwiffs and Mrs. McKinzeys - had a nice time. We stayed and went to church that night. Little Frank McKinzey went to church with us. Mr. Albott went home with Miss Kattie and Mr. Cox went home with me. Miss Fannie was left to go with little Frank. I say little. He is fourteen years old. Miss Iva went home with her pa and ma. Tuesday I spent the day with Miss Iva. That night she spent the night with me. We went

to the YPSCE meeting by our lone selves and went back by ourselves too. We would not let any of the <u>boys</u> go home with <u>us</u>. Then last Sunday Miss Ofra Carter and myself went home with Miss Iva for dinner in the afternoon. We went out riding - had a nice time. Miss May Anderson went out to Iva's for supper too and there was us three girls except Iva for supper. Miss Iva lives about a mile and a half from town. We had a nice time all day. Miss Iva spent the night with Miss Ofra Tuesday night and she and Iva came by and us three girls went to the YPSCE meeting. Mr. John Runnels went home with Ofra and Iva. Mr. Zeke Cox went with <u>me.</u> There is going to be an entertainment at the opry house tonight, but I don't think I shall go. At least my fellow hasn't been around yet. I haven't been to a picnic this summer, but take care for the <u>parties.</u>

Well, I went down to town yesterday afternoon after I came home from school and got me a new waist [blouse]. It is a cream lawn [type of material], the first cream lawn I ever saw. I think it will be very nice. I like the collar so much, Mama's making it this afternoon.

Dear Parents,

We received your letter yesterday. It does me so much good to hear from you and to hear you are both well and got plenty to eat. You said your vegetables was burning up. I can tell you they have been burned up here two months. They ship them in here from some place. If one gets them, they have to buy them so we generally do without. Pa, you asked me what we was doing for a living. We are not living much. I guess we get all we deserve. Harmon works at the carpenter trade when he can get it. When he can't get that, he does anything he can get to do. He is thirty miles from home now doing some carpenter work. It is a small job. He does good work but he is so nervous he can't get on a large house to work so his jobs don't come very often. I was glad to hear sister's [Margaret Jane] health was better. Glad also to hear John is being successful in the ministry. I do think it is one of the grandest callings that God ever gave man in this world. What has become of Nora [Margaret Jane's daughter]? She might write to a body sometimes. I guess you will think Etta don't do anything but catch beaus and go to parties. She don't go much. For the want of space I will have to quit.

Lizzie

Well, I have just finished four pages and I asked Ma how much she was going to write and she said she did not know how much she would write. I know she won't write as much as I do for she never does. Well a girl can write more than anybody so they say and especially when they are writing to their fellows (of course I don't do such but others do). There has been some sickness here this summer. Miss Fannie Smith (one of my chums) is quite ill. I haven't been to see her since Sunday afternoon. I stopped in a few minutes when we were out riding. She was getting along all right then, but I have heard from her since. She was worse the last time I heard from her. I hope she will get along all right now. Miss Mary Shirley has been sick but has started in to school. She started in yesterday morning. I had a bad cold three or four weeks ago, but it did not keep me from going to a party three miles and a half from town. I haven't saw Emma and the children in some time to talk to them. I started up there last Tuesday a week ago but haven't reached there yet. Just as I got out of sight of home, Miss Molarery came by and wanted me to go and spend the day with her, and of course I went with my old chum. Emma [Etta's sister] lives about two and a half miles out in the country on Aller Akinston place. Frank [Emma's husband] was here about ten minutes yesterday at noon. He came in town and he came by our house. Lula [William C. Jordan's daughter by his first wife] received a letter from Jewell yesterday. She said they had heard from Commodore [William C. Jordan's son by his first wife]. He is at Poolville, Texas, Parker County. Well, Ma came in and got after me for writing so much foolishness. She said that she thought that she would get to write some on this sheet. Well I guess I have written enough. Your loving little Etta.

This letter contains the voice of an 1890s thirteen-year-old who was attending school and enjoying life although her parents did not have a great deal of money to spend on her. Her account gave a picture of the activities available to young people in the 1890s.

Etta was quite a chatterbox, but her grandparents were undoubtedly pleased to get her letter. She used the polite address for her friends through much of the letter, and this was probably the proper way to write in that time period. The fact that she took the time to write to her grandparents showed the Jordan's close family ties, even among the young. Lizzie's comments in the letter concerned the continuing struggle of the Squyres family to make ends meet, but she could still laugh about the situation. Lizzie's married daughter Margaret Emma McKinney had children by the time Etta wrote this letter and lived fairly close by but out in the country. Lula, William C. Jordan's daughter by his first wife, was fourteen years old and living with the Squyres in 1895, but the reason for this remains a mystery. When did she begin to live with the Squyres? Her brother, Joseph Commodore, went by the name Commodore, and although he was a very popular member of the family, his life was filled with shadows. In later years he was a professional gambler and even reputed to have ties to the mob.[14]

A young Etta Squyres

A month later Lizzie wrote the following letter to her father.

Alvin, Texas
October 10, 1895
My dear father and mother,
    It is with the greatest of pleasure that I seat myself to answer

your most welcome letter we received last evening. I was so glad to hear from you and hear you was well and doing well.

I thank the Lord that I can hear from you and know that you are not suffering for food and rainment. Yes Pa, I think it is nice to have plenty bread stuff. Well, we are having some nice weather, cool enough to be pleasant. We had a nice rain last Sunday night. Yes, I think you can make a half a living raising poultry, and I think there isn't anything much nicer to eat than chicken and eggs. That is one luxury I haven't had since I came to Alvin. I haven't owned any chickens since we came here. I haven't lived any place where I could raise chickens.

I would give anything if I could come to see you, but I keep trying to live in hopes. Maybe the lane will turn after awhile. If it does, you will see me coming. Emma [Lizzie's daughter] lives two miles in the country. I haven't had the chance to send their letter to them yet. They was all well the other day. Fletchers [Lizzie's son] was well the last time I heard from them. Etta says tell them about her. I asked her what to tell you. She said tell you she got a prize in Sunday School for reading the most chapters in the Bible in three months. The number was seven hundred for three months. Her present was a nice Bible. Lula [William C. Jordan's daughter] said she wanted to write some this time, but she is not at home. She is as fat as a guinea pig. We was so hard run I am letting Lula stay with a lady two miles in the country at the present. She [the lady] is a very nice lady. She has no children and they have plenty. She is teaching her [Lula] at home. Lula has got a letter from Comadore, but I haven't seen it yet. When I see it, I will write and tell you what he is doing. Well, I have written all I can think of now. I remain as ever your loving daughter. Lizzie

A feeling of homesickness was evident in this letter as Lizzie was wishing she could live closer to her family. Alvin, Texas, was a long way from any of them. She not only had her own family to take care of but she also had her younger brother's child, Lula. Lizzie solved this further strain on her finances in the best way she could. She boarded Lula with a neighbor lady who could provide for her. A few years later Lula moved back to Wise County where she married Joseph Wallace Slate on January 31,

1900. She raised a large family of eight children.[15] Although the Squyres' economic situation was not good, Lizzie and Harmon were in Alvin, Texas, to stay. They would never move again,[16] whether because they were not physically or financially able to or because they liked the area around Alvin is not clear. It is also not known whether they were ever in good enough financial condition to visit their relatives in later years, or whether their family visited them in Alvin.

Lula Ella Jordan Slate in Later Years

As the turn of the century drew closer, William H. Jordan had time to sit on his porch in Percilla, Texas, on hot summer evenings and reflect upon his long life, the things he had seen come to pass, the great political events of his time, the war which had ravaged his country, the family he had watched grow and the family he had lost, the ever-changing face of the land which somehow remained timeless. He was not a man to think about accomplishments, accumulations of wealth, or even wasted opportunities. He had spent his life on the edge of the frontier, forging new trails, going new places, and starting over many times. His life had not produced a vast estate as perhaps it might

have if he had stayed in one place, but he had done his best to
protect his family and see that they had a chance to grow and
make a life for themselves. He had lived the life he chose to live,
for the most part, and on those hot summer nights in Texas at the
close of the century, he could only reflect on his contentment
with the challenges that life had offered him, and that he had met
those challenges in the best way he knew how. He had loved his
family and had honored his God. On December 20, 1895,
William H. Jordan died,[17] only six weeks after he wrote to Lizzie
that he and Martha were getting along fine. He was 78 years old,
a fairly remarkable age for a man of his generation. He was
buried at Percilla Evergreen Cemetery at Percilla, Texas[18], far
from the Georgia hills where he had been born. Years later after
the town of Percilla had ceased to exist, a devoted great grandson
erected a fine stone marker over his grave.

Chapter 22

After William died, Martha went to live with her daughter and son-in-law, Margaret Jane and John Ferguson, who farmed near Percilla, Texas. Margaret Jane's family was mostly all grown except for her youngest son, William Hugh (Willie) who was still living at home. Her son, James Walter, married Victoria Bishop in 1900.[1] Written on an old piece of school paper, the following revealed his somewhat sentimental nature, a poem that he either copied or composed himself, possibly intended for Victoria.

So well, so well, I love well.
I love you more than tongue can tell.
I love my brothers and sisters too.
But will leave them all for the sake of you.

When first you and I did part,
Grief and sorrow broke my heart.
You gave to me the parting hand,
And bade me safe to a far off land.

Now comes the rain and the snow.
The rain does fall and the wind does blow.
Some do laugh and some do cry,
And in the ground we all must lie.

Hark ye well and bear in mind,
A good friend is hard to find.
Therefore, you must, of course, remember me
And faithful ever must we be.
Walter Ferguson

Walter and Mary Ann Huddleston Ferguson
Second Wife

Margaret's daughter, Lanora (Nora), was teaching school at Crockett, Texas, from 1901 to 1902. She had finished high school and obtained a teacher's certificate because at the turn of the century, a college education was not required for a career in teaching. Teachers often boarded with families in the town where the school was located and did not have their own means of transportation. This was the case with Nora. In 1901 Margaret wrote the following letter to her daughter, Nora, at Crockett.

Lanora Bell "Nora" Ferguson

November 14, 1901
Percilla, Texas
Miss Nora Ferguson
Dear Nora,

I will try to write you a few lines this morning. I was so proud to get your letter. I never got it until Sunday morning. I thought I would write that day. I couldn't find my pencil. We are all about as usual. My cough is sometimes better and then worse.

Well, old brother and sister came Monday and stayed until yesterday. [Thomas Floyd and Willie Mae] They went to see old Grandma Lively. They promised to come back here today and stay tonight. Well, Pa is on the move, hot and heavy. I thought awhile I could not stand the thought of moving, but I have now give it up. Pa is gone now to sell and buy. He is wanting to go near Walston Spring. Floyd and wife seems willing to go. Our Willie is not going to stay here nor nowhere else so will give up to my fate, let it be what it will. I want to send for you tomorrow, but it is raining, so today I don't guess I will, but I soon will next Friday if the weather is not too bad.

Willie is gone to a wedding at Williams. One of the girls was to get married - I don't know which one. Tomie stayed with I and Grandma last night. I don't have any other ideas, but I will have to send him for you. I don't like to, but if I can't do otherwise, I will risk it.

Mr. Ray has just been home. He and Mrs. Ray was writing you a letter so I guess they will write all the news. Willie, Floyd, and the babies were here yesterday. Willie helped him get his cotton out. They have all cleaned up and turned the cows in. Write if you don't get to come.

M.J.F.

In spite of the talk of moving in this letter, the Fergusons did not move, at least not until after 1902. Margaret continued to write her daughter from Percilla, Texas, until then. Margaret and John's older children, although married and on their own, were frequent visitors and apparently lived close by. Thomas Floyd had married Willie Lively, so the references to Willie in the letter could be either Thomas's wife or Margaret Jane's youngest son

William Hugh who went by the name Willie. Thomas went by the names Tomie apparently and Floyd.

Thomas Floyd Ferguson and Willie Mae Lively Ferguson

The Fergusons' lives were consumed with neighborhood activities and the daily chores required by farming the land, not too different from the lives of their parents before them. However, the fact that the Fergusons' children were getting higher education, especially their daughter, made the children's lives different from their parents. Nora was a teacher and making her own living, something that had been possible in earlier generations, but certainly not common. Because the family was living apart from each other, transportation was a constant hassle for them. Nora did not have her own means of transportation, and even if transport were available to her, it was not safe for a young woman alone to be traveling the roads. Therefore, she was dependent upon her family to come get her if she wanted to go home, and this involved making arrangements with all the other family members. Traveling on the roads also depended upon the weather because rain and mud made horse and wagon travel difficult, if not impossible. Even though it was hard having Nora away from home and difficult transporting her back and forth,

Margaret was proud of her daughter's achievements. Her daughter was part of the new age of young people, educated and working independently from their families. These young people's accomplishments signaled the growth of the middle class workplace and a new energy in the country.

November 22, 1901
Percilla, Texas
Miss Nora Ferguson
Crockett, Texas
Dear Nora,

I received your freshest letter yesterday. It gave so much satisfaction to hear from you and hear you were doing well. I hope you will still be blessed with good health and also with good luck in your school. We are all up. My cough is no better. Pa got me a bottle of cough medicine yesterday. I do not know how it will do.

Well Nora, Pa got another letter about that box of clothes they were writing about last year. They said the box was partly packed. They wanted to know if I especially needed anything or any of the rest of the family. He sent my and your measurements. I guess we will hear from them before you go to Crockett. Willie, Brother Colwell's folks got a great lot of things, and as they said, the box was partly packed and they still had your Pa's measurements. I guess they will be apt to send it right away. He wrote back the next day. Well, some news - Mr. Hank Logan and Miss Lara Anderson got married Wednesday night at Mr. John Tipton's. I do not know the particulars of the case but things looks a little strange. Miss Anie is staying at Mr. Tipton's. Write again soon. Your loving mother

MJF
[Margaret Jane Ferguson]

Tell Mrs. Box it is grin and endure, but if we can have them all in school, we can stand that much better than having them roving like mine is wanting to do.

Because John Ferguson was an itinerant minister as well as a farmer, he and his family would occasionally receive food and clothing from church members. John and Margaret did not think of this as charity, and they were not too proud to accept such donations. Spending money on clothing was a luxury they could rarely afford, and ministers were paid little if anything. John was gone from home quite a bit with his ministerial duties, leaving Margaret and his children to run the farm. This was not easy with Margaret's unstable health. Apparently he traveled from church to church as he was needed to fill in as a temporary minister. He also performed marriages and funerals. In early 1902, John must have been concerned about his wife's deteriorating health, but the medical profession did not have many answers for lung diseases. He tried cough medicine but to no avail. His mother-in-law was not in very good health either at her advanced age.

Percilla, Texas
January 7, 1902
Miss Nora Ferguson
Crockett, Texas
Dearest Nora,

I was proud to get your letter yesterday for it seems almost like a month. I don't know that I am any better. Some days I feel all right and then worse. Grandma had another terrible spell. She reared all night. I know I never slept two hours for two nights. Grandma rested very well last night. I know half her cut up was because she got mad because I wouldn't get up and make a fire about midnight. I just told her I was not going to do it. It was no worse for her to be exposed than me. I was not, but she reared until daylight. She is making out to be mighty puny, but she don't grunt much. The rest is all well.

Willie and the children went to Palestine last Thursday and stayed until Sunday, came home on Monday morning and brought our bought goods out with them. Taxes there were 25 or 30 cents worth. I can't numerate all but will give part. Five ladies walking jackets - we have a nice one selected for you. It is a light buff I reckon is what it might be called. We gave Willie one, one for Grandma, and two for me or you. One walking dress - it is made of outing. One nice napen of worsted goods. You, I, and Pa all a nice pair of shoes, several suits of mens and boys clothes though none to fit. They think maybe they can wear a pair of pants each. Five or six shirt waists.

I want to send for you Saturday if the weather is not too bad. If it is, I will not send. I don't want you to be exposed as you have been. Your picture came New Year's Day. It is a right nice picture. It don't look as much like you as I would like though. I think of you every time I glance a look at it. It looks more like from a glance than close inspection.

Well, everybody has moved. Mr. More is our nearest neighbor. Mr. Ray is gone to Sam Pipkins place, and I can't tell all. If you don't get to come, write again soon. I am feeling all right this evening. I am so sorry for Mrs. Box. I hope Molie is better. Your mama, M.J.F.

Sometimes it was a draw as to whether Margaret or her mother felt worse. However, Margaret had reached the point in her illness that she had to protect herself first and let her mother take care of herself. She was suspicious that perhaps her mother was really just wanting attention more than that she was sick. Under other circumstances, she would have been able to give her mother the attention, but she was just too ill herself. She was still dealing with the transportation problems involved with getting her daughter home, but she was cheered by the prospect of new clothes for everyone and the receipt of her daughter's picture. Pictures were no longer on tin or some other metal but were now being made on a heavy paper similar to cardboard.

This was the last surviving letter written by Margaret Jane Ferguson. On April 30, 1902, she was very ill and finally succumbed in her long battle with lung disease.[2] She was only sixty years old. She was buried next to her father at Percilla Evergreen Cemetery. In all the years of her life, she had not changed much from the sweet, loving girl of her youth. As her brothers' confidant during the Civil War, her enthusiasm raised their spirits and kept them going. Her cooperative spirit and good natured attitude were assets for her family as well as herself. Moreover, the sadness she was forced to endure many times in her life only tempered her and made her strong. She was married to a man who moved frequently which was hard on her health and who also was gone from home quite often, leaving her the responsibility of the farm. However, she loved her family always and managed to carve her share of happiness from a sometimes harsh existence. Her love and her laughter were her legacy. The last of the generation of Jordans that had survived the American Civil War was quietly disappearing. Within fifteen to twenty years, they would all be gone.

Chapter 23

A large part of an entire generation of men was lost in the Civil War, so there were plenty of available women to marry in the years following the war. Even before the war, society allowed a man to remarry rather quickly if he lost a wife, especially if he had children to raise. Women, on the other hand, before the war were expected to observe a period of mourning before remarrying. This custom was somewhat relaxed during and after the Civil War, in many cases out of necessity. Women often had a choice of remarrying quickly or starving. After Margaret's death in 1902, John Ferguson remarried within a year to Ada Belle Crume, a woman twenty years younger than he was.[1] John was in his 60's, and Ada was around 40 years old and had never been married. This marriage produced another son for John, Harold A., born in September of 1903, the only child from this union.[2]

John's two families never did quite meld. However everyone's feelings were tempered somewhat because John's children from his marriage to Margaret were grown and had lives of their own to lead. The married children concentrated on their own families, and daughter, Nora, had reached an age where she needed to move ahead with her life. She married Samuel Augustus Crume, her new stepmother's brother, on November 19, 1903.[3] They had met through Sam's visits to his sister at Nora's father's house. Although this was probably not always a very comfortable situation for Nora with her stepmother also being her sister-in-law, her life was her own. When she was being courted by her new husband, he called her "little niece" in reference to the odd family situation in which they both found themselves.[4]

Her husband was a farmer and came from an established family living in Cherokee County, Texas. He was also a widower with a young son. His first wife had died young along with their two-year-old son and an infant. He was left to raise his four-year-old son by himself, and he proved himself remarkably resilient and equal to the situation. By 1903 when he married Nora, the four-year-old was eight, and Gus, as he was known, was almost ten years older than Nora. However, he had a good sense of humor, and they shared laughter often.[5] All of their complicated family relationships were not as important as their love for and commitment to each other.

Samuel Agustus Crume

Nora's younger brother, Willie, followed her in marriage on November 9, 1905. He married Louella "Ella" Featherstone who would be his perfect partner with her down-to-earth practicality.[6]

William Hugh "Willie" and Louella "Ella" Ferguson

This marriage left none of John Ferguson's children by his first marriage still living at home. This was probably just as well. John and Ada Belle were able to concentrate on raising their son, but still interacted with the children and grandchildren from John's first marriage. They had fourteen years together before John Ferguson died in 1916. He was buried beside his first wife, Margaret Jane, and his father-in-law, W. H. Jordan, at Percilla Evergreen Cemetery at Percilla, Texas. Ada Belle never remarried; she was content to raise her son alone. Years later when Ada Belle died, she was buried at Percilla beside John, on his other side.[8]

After John's death, his two families continued to disagree at times over the land he owned and its mineral rights. Because John's second wife survived him, she received the majority of the mineral rights shares and passed them on to her son. The other side of the family felt that because their mother had done much of the work on the farm while John was gone as an itinerant preacher, that this was not fair.[7] Fair or not, the distribution of mineral rights shares was determined by the laws of Texas.

It seems unusual that the Fergusons were not buried at Alder Branch in the Ferguson Cemetery, especially since it was not too far away. However, W. H. Jordan died first and was buried at Percilla, and this may have set a pattern. His daughter, Margaret, died next and she may have wanted to be buried next to her father, and when John's turn came, he wanted to be buried next to his first wife. And so on, it may have gone. Other Ferguson family members were buried at Percilla Evergreen thereafter.

When Margaret Jane died in 1902 and John remarried, it no longer seemed appropriate for Martha Jordan to continue to live on the Ferguson farm. Therefore, she moved to the home of her daughter, Martha Huddleston, in Wise County, Texas. She lived there a few years until she became ill and died on March 27, 1905. She was buried at Bethel Cemetery next to two of the Huddleston children who had died young.[9] She had lived a life which was always changing because the war had destroyed the familiar existence she had known in the South and her husband could not seem to stay in one place for long. She outlived most of her children, not a circumstance she would have chosen and one that caused her a great amount of sadness. However, she loved her family and found her own peace with the life she had been given. She died and was buried in the West, far from where she had begun her life, in more ways than one.

The children of William and Martha Jordan that remained in 1905 were also gone within fifteen to twenty years. Martha Huddleston died in September of 1917 at age 65, and her husband, Dan, only outlived her by five years, passing in January of 1922. They left behind a large family of sons, one daughter, and many grandchildren. Their life in Wise Co., Texas, was the most stable of all the Jordan families' lives because they stayed in one place. They were buried at Bethel Cemetery in Wise County, Texas, next to Martha Jordan and their two young children who had died previously.[10] Harmon Squyres died on July 6, 1916, and Mary Elizabeth (Lizzie) went to live with her daughter Etta and husband. Lizzie died on May 16, 1928 at age 87.[11] She was the last Jordan of her generation in the William H. Jordan line and the only one to live to an advanced age, which was somewhat remarkable because of the hard life that she had lived. Harmon was only able to make a marginal living with his part time carpentry work and farming, and the family barely survived at times. The Squyres were buried in the Confederate Cemetery at Alvin, Texas, along with their son, William Fletcher and grandson Carlos. Their daughters and grandchildren continued the family line into the decades that followed.

Jordan Land, Deming, New Mexico

Lizzie's brother, Perry Jordan, William Jordan's last living son, had continued his farming and other occupations into the new century. Part of the years up until 1910 he and some of his family lived in Oklahoma in Greer Co. at Looney, Oklahoma. He may have moved to the southern New Mexico area at Deming just prior to 1910 because some of his children were living there, but perhaps not. Several of his children and their families stayed in Oklahoma permanently.[12] Others moved to northern New Mexico near Gladstone and later lived in the Albuquerque area. On March 21, 1910, Perry died at age 61, and the circumstances of his death were highly unusual.

The story is told by his descendants that he had been on his way by train to Washington, D.C. to patent a farming equipment invention. He apparently got too friendly with some men on the train and was later found in New Orleans badly beaten. He was taken to the Soniat Leonce Memorial Mercy Hospital (now closed and not in use) where he was cared for by the Sisters of Mercy.[13] Before the beating, Perry had apparently contracted a strep infection on his face called erysipilis. This strep infection could be deadly, antibiotics were not available, and so it ran its course in Perry's case according to the death certificate. He died of it combined with pneumonia and the beating.[14]

He was buried in New Orleans in a cemetery for the indigent and also one of the few cemeteries in New Orleans where the dead were buried underground.[15] Eventually the gravesite was covered over by a white marble mausoleum where others were buried. In New Orleans it was and still is the custom to bury people in layers or levels in each plot or crypt at the cemetery. According to family members, a few months after Perry's death, a large company came out with the same invention that he was promoting. A shoe box containing a bloody shirt, shoes, and some personal items was shipped back to his son, Charles Franklin Jordan, at Deming, New Mexico.[16] It was a bizarre ending for the last Jordan man of his generation, but none of the Jordan men in this generation had been fortunate in having long lives.

Mary Ann, Perry's wife, was staying with her youngest son's family at Deming in southern New Mexico, either because of

Perry's death or because the two families were living together on the same farm/ranch. Mary Ann, who was already having mental problems according to her descendants, lost her mind completely after Perry's death. She could not be trusted around young children, so she eventually left her youngest son's home and went to live with several of her older children in northern New Mexico. Twenty years after her husband, Mary Ann Jordan died on November 24, 1931, at Gladstone, New Mexico, and was buried there.[17] She was the only member of the family to be buried at Gladstone, even though several of Perry's children lived in the Gladstone area, not always at the same time, and then moved on.

Land near Gladstone, New Mexico

Gladstone, New Mexico, was wide-open ranching country, an example of the Old West that was much heralded in books and eventually movies and television. Miles of rolling grasslands interspersed with some stretches of cactus and sagebrush made an appealing place to raise cattle, and there were enough people who lived on the ranches in the area to provide some sense of community and social life.[18]

The fact that Perry Jordan was interested in inventions made him a man of his times because so many new inventions came on the market after the turn of the century. The telephone began to replace the popularity of the personal letter, the automobile replaced the horse and wagon, and eventually people even flew through the air in an airplane. These inventions in turn produced other changes in people's everyday lives such as paved roads, different wearing apparel, and wires running all over the countryside. Electricity and indoor bathrooms came about also. It was a whole new world.[19]

By 1930, William and Martha Jordan and their children, their pain and their laughter, belonged to the past, to the family history, but their grandchildren were already living their contribution to the family record. New voices in letters written to the family members were preserving the next generation's story. One of these voices was Margaret Jane Ferguson's only daughter, Lanora Belle, to whom Margaret passed on the family letters and keepsakes. It was Nora's turn to be the keeper of the past and add her voice to those who had gone before. Her letters and those of her children were being saved with the family keepsakes to be passed on. A new journey was begun.

Chapter 24

"Well, Mom," I asked, "Do you think these Jordans were like us?"

Mom laughed, "Yes, I do, but it works both ways. We are like them as well. In a lot of ways we are different from them because we don't live in the same time or place, but in some ways we are the same."

"Whaddya mean?" I persisted.

"Well, we don't have the health problems that they did because of lack of medicine, spoiled food, and poor housing, but we have our own illnesses caused by living in today's world. Although today we don't often die of the diseases that killed people in the Jordans' time such as flu and measles, we are still sick quite frequently, so illness is still a part of our lives. And today we have killer diseases that the Jordans did not have to worry about. Our family hasn't moved as much as they did, and we haven't lived through a war in our backyard. However, we have had our own challenges in the twentieth century that require strength, ingenuity, and flexibility. We have fought in wars, and our society as a whole has continued to be a mobile one. In those ways we are the same. We have more education and we think we know more, but in some areas, they may have known more and been wiser. They valued people more than things. Most importantly, we have a sense of humor, a belief in God, a love of family, and a stubborn will to survive and thrive just like they did."

Although I couldn't understand all the big words or ideas, my imagination was humming. "I wish we could see them and talk to them for awhile. I bet they could tell some wild stories," I figured.

"They already have," my mother said. "Because they saved the family letters and passed them down through generations of people to us, we are able to listen to their stories. Although they didn't realize it at the time, they made sure we would have the chance to know them a hundred years forward in time. They weren't philosophers or great writers, but the way they wrote about the simple, everyday things that made up their lives revealed a lot about them. In their voices we can sometimes hear ourselves and perhaps know ourselves."

"That's pretty cool," I said. "Do you think they would have liked us if they could have met us?"

"Darling girl," Mom threw her arms around me and hugged me. "They would have loved us! We are family, and other than God, family was the most important thing in their lives, and it links us to them even today. They would have loved us."

Author's Notes

The family information contained in this book is accurate and consistent with what the author has been able to discover up to the present moment. There is more than likely much more to know, but that is the nature of family research. One more tidbit of information is always waiting out there in a dusty old tome ready to be discovered, a tantalizing idea that teases the researcher to distraction. However, at some point, what is known needs to be recorded on paper to be preserved, and that is one of the purposes of this book. This is my contribution to the pieces of the Jordan puzzle, a truly fascinating journey.

The old letters contained in this book were edited for spelling and punctuation in order to make them easier to read. Grammar and word choice were left alone. For those readers who are curious about the original appearance of the letters and who wish to try deciphering them, copies of several of the original letters have been included. The names in the letters have not been changed in any way, so it may be possible for some readers to find a reference to a long-lost relative. Have fun!

The bibliography/notes pages at the end of the book probably do not include all of the multitude of public documents, research material from genealogists, Bible records, obituaries, cemetery records, etc. which went into the research for this book. The author tried to include as many as possible. I am indebted to many libraries/archives across the country for their generous help. A special thank you goes to the many genealogists/family researchers who have helped with this project. Without your help, this book would not be as complete as it is. Thanks so much. Thanks as well to the two gentlemen who helped me restore the Jordan ambrotypes and photographs, a long and tiresome project, Rex Heinitz and S.C. Dixon.

Because a project of this nature is never truly complete and the scope of the book was confined to the people who wrote the old letters, anyone seeking more information about the Jordan families or who would like to contribute to their story is welcome to contact me. All of the Jordan men of 1820 Brookhaven, Mississippi, are thought to be related, but no definitive proof has been found of their relationship. In trying to find the relationship, I have also researched other families to a limited degree who married into the Jordan family, especially in the Gray Jordan time period, the Bristers, Chandlers, Suttons, Harts, Prices and others. The Jordans in North Carolina have yet to be discovered, and there are family rumors of pirates in that bunch, so my Jordan journey will continue for a while longer. Some work has been done on the North Carolina Jordans in 2009 through DNA studies and other means, but there is much left to do.

Notes and Sources

Chapter 2

1. Gladow research trips to Brookhaven, Mississippi, and Bienville Parish, Louisiana, 2001.
2. Bible record of Simeon Jordan, Gray Jordan's son. The Bible can be accessed through Pam Stone, a descendant.
3. Franklin Co., Georgia marriage records and Simeon Jordan's Bible record.
4. Lawrence County, Mississippi tax records for the year 1818.
5. "Lawrence County History, Chapter 1." 11 August 1999. Page 2. <http://www.rootsweb.com/~msjdavis/jdhis_form.html>
6. Hobbs, Henry Ware. "History of Brookhaven, Mississippi." The Daily Leader. 1992. Reprinted Newcomer Magazine. 2001: 25. Mrs. Nancy Methvin. Personal Interview. 1999.
7. Hart, Royce. Aspects of the Hart Family History. Brookhaven, Mississippi: self published, 1983.
8. Hobbs, Henry Ware. "History of Brookhaven, Mississippi." The Daily Leader. 1992. Reprinted Newcomer Magazine. 2001: 25.
9. Hobbs, Henry Ware. "History of Brookhaven, Mississippi." The Daily Leader. 1992. Reprinted Newcomer Magazine. 2001: 25.
10. Federal census records for Lawrence County, Mississippi 1820-1850.
11. Federal census records for Lawrence County, Mississippi 1820-1860. Simeon Jordan's Bible record.
12. Federal census records for Lawrence County, Mississippi 1820-1860. Cemetery records for Lincoln County, Mississippi and Rapides Parish, Louisiana.
13. Marriage records for Lawrence County, Mississippi. Federal census records for Lawrence County, Mississippi 1820-1860. Bible records from Margaret Jane Jordan Ferguson and Martha Ann Jordan Huddleston.

14. Birth dates of the William and Wyatt Jordan children determined when the families moved to Louisiana. All federal census records on the two families between 1850 and 1870 are either lost or nonexistent. Julie Ann Jordan's birth place of Meridian, Mississippi, provided by her descendants.

15. 1850 Federal Census for Claiborne Parish, Louisiana.

16. Kleinpeter, Sharon O. "History of Bienville Parish, Louisiana." 31 December 1997.
    <http://www.rootsweb.com/~labienvi/histor~1.htm>

17. Kleinpeter, Sharon O. "History of Bienville Parish, Louisiana." 31 December 1997.
    <http://www.rootsweb.com/~labienvi/histor~1.htm>

18. Land and tax records for Bienville Parish, Louisiana.

19. Gladow research trip to Bienville Parish, Louisiana, 2001.

20. Land records from Bienville Parish, Louisiana.

21. Federal census record for Lawrence County, Mississippi 1850.

22. Marriage records for Lawrence County, Mississippi.

23. Hobbs, Henry Ware. "History of Brookhaven, Mississippi." The Daily Leader. 1992. Reprinted Newcomer Magazine. 2001: 25.

24. Federal census records for Lawrence County, Mississippi 1860.

25. "Margaret Jordan Bill of Complaint." Monticello, MS: Southern District Chancery Court, Lawrence Co., MS, District of Monticello, 1853.

26. "Margaret Jordan vs. Gray Jordan, no. 125, Gray Jordan's Response to Bill of Complaint." Monticello, MS: Southern District Chancery Court, Lawrence Co., MS, District of Monticello, 11 Nov. 1853.

27. "Indenture Articles, Margaret Jordan vs. Gray Jordan, no. 125" Monticello, MS: Southern District Chancery Court, Lawrence Co., MS, District of Monticello, 14 Jan. 1854.

28. Federal Census record for Lawrence County, Mississippi 1860.

29. Mr. and Mrs. Bob Coke of Brookhaven, Mississippi. Personal Interview. August 2005.

30. Federal census record for Henderson County, Texas 1870.

31. Marriage records for Bienville Parish, Louisiana.

Chapter 3
1. Floyd H. Jordan Military Records. Washington, D.C.: National Archives and Records Service. General Services Administration. 1861-1862.
2. Camp Moore Confederate Museum and Cemetery Visitors' Guide. Tangipahoa, Louisiana: Camp Moore Historical Association, Inc.
3. "Camp Moore History." 22 July 1998. <http://ourworld.compuserve.com/homepages/forrest64/history.htm>
4. "Medical Care, Battle Wounds, and Disease." 4 July 2000. Original source: The Civil War Society's "Encyclopedia of the Civil War." <http://www.civilwarhome.com/civilwarmedicine.htm>
5. Camp Moore Confederate Museum and Cemetery Visitor's Guide. Tangipahoa, Louisiana: Camp Moore Historical Association, Inc.
6. Floyd H. Jordan. Letter to his sister, Margaret Jane Jordan. 6 August 1861. Gladow private collection.
7. "Medical Care, Battle Wounds, and Disease." 4 July 2000. Original source: The Civil War Society's "Encyclopedia of the Civil War." <http://www.civilwarhome.com/civilwarmedicine.htm>
8. Bergeron, Arthur W. Jr. "9th Regiment Louisiana Infantry." <u>Guide to Louisiana Confederate</u> email to: joec6718@ix.netcom.com. <u>Military Units 1861-1865.</u> Baton Rouge: LSU Press, 1989.

Chapter 4
1. "Medical Care, Battle Wounds, and Disease." 4 July 2000. Original source: The Civil War Society's "Encyclopedia of the Civil War." <http://www.civilwarhome.com/camplife.htm>
2. "Life in a Civil War Army Camp." 30 April 2006. Original Source: The Civil War Society's "Encyclopedia of the Civil War." <http://www.civilwarhome.com/camplife.htm>
3. "Life in a Civil War Army Camp." 30 April 2006. Original

Source: The Civil War Society's "Encyclopedia of the Civil War." <http://www.civilwarhome.com/camplife.htm>

Chapter 5
1. "Floyd H. Jordan Military Records." Washington, D.C.: National Archives and Records Service. General Services Administration.
2. "Floyd H. Jordan Military Records." Washington, D.C.: National Archives and Records Service. General Services Administration.
3. "Floyd H. Jordan Military Records." Washington, D.C.: National Archives and Records Service. General Services Administration.
4. "James M. and Wyatt Jordan Military Records." Washington, D.C.: National Archives and Records Service. General Services Administration.
5. "George Bates Military Records." Washington, D.C.: National Archives and Records Service. General Services Administration.
6. "Wyatt Jordan Military Records." Washington, D.C.: National Archives and Records Service. General Services Administration.
7. "W. Jordan Cemetery Record." Charlottesville, Virginia: Soldiers Cemetery University of Virginia.
8. "Simeon Jordan Military Records." Washington D.C.: National Archives and Records Service. General Services Administration.
   "Johnson Guards' Company C Lawrence County." 33rd Mississippi Infantry Regiment. July 25, 2001. http://msnhomepages.talkcity.com/LaGrangeLn/davidg33/
9. "Johnson Guards' Company C Lawrence County." 33rd Mississippi Infantry Regiment. July 25, 2001. http://msnhomepages.talkcity.com/LaGrangeLn/davidg33/
10. "Tragedy Writes its Name on Confederate Soldiers Home." Daily Herald [Biloxi, MS] 16 December 1924: 1-2
11. Hobbs, Henry Ware. "History of Brookhaven, Mississippi." The Daily Leader. 1992. Reprinted Newcomer Magazine. 2001: 37.

Chapter 6
1. "Floyd H. Jordan Military Records." Washington, D.C.: National Archives and Records Service. General Services Administration.
2. "Front Royal." Civil War Battle Summaries. <u>American Battlefield Protection Program.</u> National Park Service. 19 June 2000. http://www2.cr.nps.gov/abpp/battles/va103.htm
3. "First Winchester." Civil War Battle Summaries. <u>American Battlefield Protection Program.</u> National Park Service. 19 June 2000. http://www2.cr.nps.gov/abpp/battles/va104.htm.
4. "Cross Keys." Civil War Battle Summaries. <u>American Battlefield Protection Program.</u> National Park Service. 19 June 2000. http://www2.cr.nps.gov/abpp/battles/va105.htm.
5. "Port Republic." Civil War Battle Summaries. <u>American Battlefield Protection Program.</u> National Park Service. 19 June 2000. http://www2.cr.nps.gov/abpp/battles/va106.htm
6. "Malvern Hill." Civil War Battle Summaries. <u>American Battlefield Protection Program.</u> National Park Service. 19 June 2000. http://www2.cr.nps.gov/abpp/battles/va021.htm
7. Bergeron, Arthur W. Jr. "9th Regiment Louisiana Infantry." <u>Guide to Louisiana Confederate Military Units 1861-1865.</u> Baton Rouge: LSU Press, 1989.
8. "Malvern Hill." Civil War Battle Summaries. <u>American Battlefield Protection Program.</u> National Park Service. 19 June 2000. http://www2.cr.nps.gov/abpp/battles/va021.htm
9. Bergeron, Arthur W. Jr. "9th Regiment Louisiana Infantry." <u>Guide to Louisiana Confederate Military Units 1861-1865.</u> Baton Rouge: LSU Press, 1989.
10. "Cedar Mountain." Civil War Batttle Summaries. <u>American Battlefield Protection Program.</u> National Park Service. 19 June 2000. http://www2.cr.nps.gov/abpp/battles/va022.htm
11. Bergeron, Arthur W. Jr. <u>Guide to Louisiana Confederate Military Units 1861-1865.</u> Baton Rouge: LSU Press, 1989. Page 94.
12. "Second Manassas." Civil War Battle Summaries. <u>American Battlefield Protection Program.</u> National Park Service. 19 June 2000. http://www2.cr.nps.gov/abpp/battles/va026.htm

Chapter 7

1. "James M. Jordan Military Records." Washington D.C.: National Archives and Records Service. General Services Administration.

2. "A Civil War Hospital Center." Confederate Hospitals in Lynchburg Virginia. 17 October 1999.
   http://www.lynchburgbiz.com/occ/CivilWar/cwhospitals.html

3. "James M. Jordan Military Records." Washington D.C.: National Archives and Records Service. General Services Administration. Also letter from Floyd Jordan to his family 1862. Gladow private collection.

4. "The Confederate Section in the Old City Cemetery." 17 October 1999.
   http://www.lynchburgbiz.com/occ/CivilWar/Confederate.html

5. "Harpers Ferry." Civil War Battle Summaries. American Battlefield Protection Program. National Park Service. 19 June 2000. http://www2.cr.nps.gov/abpp/battles/wv010.htm

6. Davis, William C. "Jack." Civil War Parks: The Story Behind the Scenery. Las Vegas, NV: KC Publications, Inc. 1984.

7. "Report of Col. Leroy A. Stafford, 9th Louisiana Infantry, of operations August 31- October 5." The War of the Rebellion: A Compilation of the Official Records of the Union and Confederate Armies. The Civil War CD-Rom: The War of the Rebellion. Carmel, Indiana: Guild Press of Indiana, Inc.,2000. Series I-Volume XIX/1 (S#27). No. 291.

8. "Antietam." Civil War Battle Summaries. American Battlefield Protection Program. National Park Service. 19 June 2000. http://ww2.cr.nps.gov/abpp/battles/md003.htm

9. "Report of Col. Leroy A. Stafford, 9th Louisiana Infantry, of operations August 31-October 5." The War of the Rebellion: A Compilation of the Official Records of the Union and Confederate Armies. The Civil War CD-Rom: The War of the Rebellion. Carmel, Indiana: Guild Press of Indiana, Inc., 2000. Series I-Volume XIX/1 (S#27). No. 291.

10. "Antietam." Civil War Battle Summaries. American Battlefield Protection Program. National Park Service. 19 June 2000. http://ww2.cr.nps.gov/abpp/battles/md003.htm

11. Davis, William C. "Jack." Civil War Parks:The Story Behind

<u>the Scenery.</u> Las Vegas, NV: KC Publications, Inc. 1984.

12. Bergeron, Arthur W. Jr. "9th Regiment Louisiana Infantry." <u>Guide to Louisiana Confederate Military Units 1861-1865.</u> Baton Rouge: LSU Press, 1989.

13. Bergeron, Arthur W. Jr. "9th Regiment Louisiana Infantry." <u>Guide to Louisiana Confederate Military Units 1861-1865.</u> Baton Rouge: LSU Press, 1989.

14. "Floyd H. Jordan Military Records." Washington D.C.: National Archives and Records Service. General Services Administration.

15. "Floyd H. Jordan Military Records." Washington D.C.: National Archives and Records Service. General Services Administration.

16. Bergeron, Arthur W. Jr. "9th Regiment Louisiana Infantry." <u>Guide to Louisiana Confederate Military Units 1861-1865.</u> Baton Rouge: LSU Press, 1989.

17. "The Civil War in Louisiana: An Overview." 31 December 1997.
http://www.crt.state.la.us/crt/tourism/civilwar/overview.htm

18. "Company H, Brush Valley Guards, Bienville Parish, 9th Louisiana Infantry Regiment, CSA." Ninth Infantry Regiment Louisiana Volunteers. 29 May 2008.
http://tcc230.tripod.com/CoH9thLa.htm.

Chapter 9

1. "The Civil War in Louisiana: An Overview." 31 December 1997.
http://www.crt.state.la.us/crt/tourism/civilwar/overview.htm

2. "W.H. Jordan Land Sale Record." Arcadia, Louisiana: Bienville Parish Clerk Records. Property deeded on 27 August 1863. Recorded in Conveyance Book EE, page 78.

3. "Gray Jordan Estate Records." Monticello, Mississippi: Lawrence Co. Miss. Chancery Court Records. Box 36. Death date listed as 18 September 1863 in the initial petition.

4. Family letters from W.H. Jordan family in Texas to Martha Jordan in Louisiana. Gladow private collection.

5. "The Civil War in Louisiana: An Overview." 31 December 1997.

http://www.crt.state.la.us/crt/tourism/civilwar/overview.htm
6. Gladow research trip to the Palestine, Texas area. 2000.
7. "A Partial History of Anderson County, Texas." 14 January 2001. http://www.tvec.net/~bonniew/acgs/hist.htm.
8. Blum, Catton, Morgan, Schlesinger, Stampp, and Woodward. The National Experience. New York: Harcourt and Brace, 1963. Pages 348-350.

Chapter 10
1. "The Civil War in Louisiana: An Overview." 31 December 1997.
   http://www.crt.state.la.us/crt/tourism/civilwar/overview.htm
2. Many sources may be found on this subject at http://www.cwc.lsu.edu/cwc/links/links7.htm
3. A general discussion of economics in the South during and after the Civil War can be found in Blum, Catton, Morgan, Schlesinger, Stampp, and Woodward. The National Experience. New York: Harcourt and Brace, 1963. Pages 356-392. http://www.civilwarhome.com/camplife.htm. "The Civil War in Louisiana: An Overview." 31 December 1997. http://www.crt.state.la.us/crt/tourism/civilwar/overview.htm

Chapter 11
1. "Mansfield Sabine Crossroads, Pleasant Grove, Louisiana." American Civil War, April 8, 1864. February 15, 1999. http://americancivilwar.com/statepic/la/la018.html
2. "Report of Col. Leroy A. Stafford, 9th Louisiana Infantry, of operations August 31-October 5." The War of the Rebellion: A Compilation of the Official Records of the Union and Confederate Armies. The Civil War CD-Rom: The War of the Rebellion. Carmel, Indiana: Guild Press of Indiana, Inc., 2000. Series I-Volume XIX/1 (S#27). No. 291.
3. Stone monuments at the Pleasant Hill, Louisiana, battle and cemetery memorial site near Mansfield, Louisiana.
4. "The Civil War in Louisiana: An Overview." 31 December 1997.
   http://www.crt.state.la.us/crt/tourism/civilwar/overview.htm
5. "Pleasant Hill Louisiana." American Civil War, April 9, 1864.

February 15, 1999.
http://americancivilwar.com/statepic/la/la019.html

6. Stone monuments at the Pleasant Hill, Louisiana battle and cemetery memorial site near Mansfield, Louisiana.

Chapter 12

1. Various articles from the Bienville Messenger. Vol. 1, No. 1-52, 21 Oct 1865-13 Oct 1866. September 9, 1999. ftp://ftp.rootsweb.com/put/usgenweb/la/bienville/misc/oldbn.t xt

2. "The Civil War in Louisiana: An Overview." 31 December 1997. http://www.crt.state.la.us/crt/tourism/civilwar/overview.htm

3. Blum, Catton, Morgan, Schlesinger, Stampp, and Woodward. The National Experience. New York: Harcourt and Brace, 1963. Page 353.

4. "The Civil War in Louisiana: An Overview." 31 December 1997. http://www.crt.state.la.us/crt/tourism/civilwar/overview.htm

5. George Bates Military Records. Washington, D.C.: National Archives and Records Service. General Services Administration.

6. "The Civil War in Louisiana: An Overview." 31 December 1997. http://www.crt.state.la.us/crt/tourism/civilwar/overview.htm

7. Pioneer Families of Anderson County Prior to 1900. Palestine, Texas: Anderson County Genealogical Society, September 1984. Pages 127-8, 186-7, 349-351.

8. Hassell, W.J., Wolf, Kay, and Sadorf, Virginia. "William 'King' David Ferguson." Pioneer Families of Anderson County Prior to 1900. Palestine, Texas: Anderson County Genealogical Society, September 1984. Pages 127-8.

9. Hassell, W.J., Wolf, Kay, and Sadorf, Virginia. "William 'King' David Ferguson." Pioneer Families of Anderson County Prior to 1900. Palestine, Texas: Anderson County Genealogical Society, September 1984. Pages 127-8.

10. Hudddleston, Patricia Cook. "Huddleston." Pioneer Families of Anderson County Prior to 1900. Palestine, Texas: Anderson

County Genealogical Society, September 1984. Pages 186-88.

11. Squyres, Fred and Ruby. "Squyres." Pioneer Families of Anderson County Prior to 1900. Palestine, Texas: Anderson County Genealogical Society, September 1984. Pages 349-351.

12. General Index to Marriages 1846-1900. Palestine, Anderson County, Texas.

13. General Index to Marriages 1846-1900. Palestine, Anderson County, Texas.

14. Harmon V. Squyres Military Records. Washington, D.C.: National Archives and Records Service. General Services Administration. Also, the pension application of Squyres has some of his Civil War military record.

15. 1870 Federal Census Records. Anderson and Henderson Counties, Texas.

16. Henderson County, Texas Tax Rolls 1846-1903. Arlington, Texas: University of Texas at Arlington, #110701 and #110702. Also Henderson County, Texas Voters' Registration 1867-1872.
http://www.rootsweb.com/~txhender/hevoters67.html.

Chapter 13

1. Gladow research trip to Henderson County, Texas in March 2000.

2. Goodrow, Mrs. Ray. "Brief History of Anderson County." Pioneer Families of Anderson County Prior to 1900. Palestine, Texas: Anderson County Genealogical Society, September 1984. Pages ix-xi.

3. "A Partial History of Anderson County, Texas." 14 January 2001. http://www.tvec.net/~bonniew/acgs/hist.htm. Sources of the article are given at the beginning.

4. 1870 Federal Census Record for Henderson and Anderson Counties, Texas. Also tax records for Henderson and Anderson Counties.

5. 1870 Federal Census Record for Anderson County, Texas.

6. Henderson County, Texas Marriage Records. Bible record marriage certificate dated December 7, 1869. Bible is owned by the Huddleston family and was probably Martha Ann

Jordan Huddleston's.

7. 1870 Federal Census Record for Henderson County, Texas.
8. Estate Records for Wyatt Jordan. Bienville Parish Clerk's Office. Arcadia, Louisiana. Record #1269.
9. Marriage records for Bienville Parish, Louisiana.
10. Federal census records for 1870-1900 in Hood and Henderson Counties and other county records such as court and marriage in Hood County.

Chapter 14

1. Blum, Catton, Morgan, Schlesinger, Stampp, and Woodward. The National Experience. New York: Harcourt and Brace, 1963. Page 358.
2. Camp Moore Confederate Museum and Cemetery Visitor's Guide. Tangipahoa, Louisiana: Camp Moore Historical Association, Inc.
3. Gray Jordan Probate Records. Lawrence County Clerk's Office. Monticello, Mississippi.
4. Hobbs, Henry Ware. "History of Brookhaven, Mississippi." The Daily Leader. 1992. Reprinted Newcomer Magazine. 2001: 37-38.
5. Report of U.S. Grant to Major General Halleck on May 6, 1863. The War of the Rebellion: A Compilation of the Official Records of the Union and Confederate Armies. The Civil War CD-Rom: The War of the Rebellion. Carmel, Indiana: Guild Press of Indiana, Inc., 2000.
6. Hobbs, Henry Ware. "History of Brookhaven, Mississippi." The Daily Leader. 1992. Reprinted Newcomer Magazine. 2001: 37-38.
7. 1870-1880 Federal Census Records for Lincoln County, Mississippi.
8. Hobbs, Henry Ware. "History of Brookhaven, Mississippi." The Daily Leader. 1992. Reprinted Newcomer Magazine. 2001: 37-38.
9. "Simeon Jordan, 3rd Corporal/Musician." Lincoln County Times. Brookhaven, Mississippi. March 3, 1927.

Chapter 15

1. Anderson County Tax Rolls 1846-1902. Huntsville, Texas: Sam Houston State University. Reel #100101-100104.
2. Jordan family letters written from 1870-1900. Gladow private collection. Also county tax rolls for various counties in Texas (See citations for counties previously mentioned.).
3. Federal census records for 1870 and 1880 in Anderson, Henderson, and Hood Counties, Texas.
4. Cherokee County, Texas marriage records. Rusk, Texas.
5. Joan Singletary (Fondren researcher) and Barbara Yancy Hall (Perry Jordan descendant) research.
6. Handbook of Texas Online, s.v., http://www.tsha.utexas.edu/handbook/online/articles/CC/hcc1 0.html (accessed August 9, 2007).
7. 1840 Federal Census for Lawrence County, Mississippi; 1850 Federal Census for Cherokee Co., Texas.
8. Henderson County, Texas Tax Rolls 1846-1903. Arlington, Texas: University of Texas at Arlington. Reel #110701 and 110702.

Chapter 16

1. Federal Census record for 1880 Navarro County, Texas.
2. Blum, Catton, Morgan, Schlesinger, Stampp, and Woodward. The National Experience. New York: Harcourt and Brace, 1963. Page 482.
3. Federal Census record for 1880 Navarro County, Texas and tax rolls for Cherokee County, Texas.
4. Joan Singletary, Fondren research.
5. Navarro County, Texas marriage records.
6. Federal Census record for 1880 Navarro County, Texas and tax rolls for Cherokee County, Texas.
7. Federal Census record for 1880 Navarro County, Texas.
8. Federal Census record for 1880 Navarro County, Texas.
9. Gladow research trip in March 2000.
10. C Jester,.L. "A Short History of Navarro County, Texas and Corsica." Navarro County, Texas GenWeb site. 13 September 2006. www.rootsweb.com/~txnavarr/county_history/short_history.htm

11. Anderson County Genealogical Society. "A Partial History of Anderson County, Texas." 14 January 2001. http://www.tvec.net/~bonniew/acgs/hist.htm

12. Kerr, K. Austin. "Prohibition." The Handbook of Texas Online. 6 July 2002. http://www.tsha.utexas.edu/handbook/online/articles/print/PP/vap1.html

13. Social Security application and death certificate of Joseph Commodore Jordan.

14. Federal Census for 1880 Navarro County, Anderson County, and Wise County, Texas.

15. Tax Rolls for Navarro County, Hood County, and Wise County, Texas.

Chapter 18

1. Gladow research trip to Texas. October 2000.

2. "Hood County." The Handbook of Texas Online. (Accessed Aug. 6, 2000). http://www.tsha.utexas.edu/handbook/online/articles/view/HH/hch17.html

3. Hood County, Texas tax records. GenWeb site for Hood County, Texas. (Accessed Aug. 6, 2000).

4. Gladow private collection of family letters and papers.

5. Huddleston Family Bible. Julia Huddleston Mosely researcher.

6. Federal Census for 1900 Brazoria County, Texas.

7. Federal Census for 1880 Wise County, Texas

8. Barbara Stear research on Perry Jordan family.

9. Penny Holmes research on William C. Jordan family.

10. Penny Holmes research on William C. Jordan family.

11. Penny Holmes research on William C. Jordan family.

12. Penny Holmes research on William C. Jordan family.

13. Gladow research trip in March 2000.

14. Wise Co., Texas tax records.

15. "The Great Western Trail Through Texas." Brochure created by the Wilbarger County Historical Commission and the Red River Valley Museum. 2004.

16. Wilbarger County, Texas land records. Vernon, Texas.

17. Huddleston Family Bible. Julia Huddleston Mosely

researcher.

18. Barbara Stear research on Perry Jordan family.

19. Ferguson Family Research. Laura C. Broughton. 1960.

20. Hood County, Texas marriage records.

21. Family research from Lissa Johnston and Barbara Muphey-Taylor.

Chapter 19

1. "Texas History."
   wysiwyg://17/http://www.thecitiesof.com/texas/escape/texashi
   story.html (Accessed July 6, 2002, 1:17 p.m. US Central)
   Blum, Catton, Morgan, Schlesinger, Stampp, andWoodward.
   The National Experience. New York: Harcourt and Brace,
   1963.

2. "19th Century Education in America."
   http://kclibrary.nhmccd.edu/19thcentury1850.htm
   (Accessed August 13, 2007, 4:45 p.m. US Central)
   Blum, Catton, Morgan, Schlesinger, Stampp, and Woodward.
   The National Experience. New York: Harcourt and Brace,
   1963.

Chapter 20

1. Blum, Catton, Morgan, Schlesinger, Stampp, and Woodward.
   The National Experience. New York: Harcourt and Brace,
   1963. Pages 418-424.

2. "Prohibition." The Handbook of Texas Online. (Accessed July
   6, 2002).
   http://www.tsha.utexas.edu/handbook/online/articles/view/PP/
   vap1.html

3. Blum, Catton, Morgan, Schlesinger, Stampp, and Woodward.
   The National Experience. New York: Harcourt and Brace,
   1963. Page 453.

Chapter 21

1. Wise Co. and Houston Co., Texas tax records.

2. Lillian Lena Jordan Miller family Bible record.

3. Wilbarger Co. Texas land records, Vernon, Texas.

4. Wilbarger Co. Texas land records, Vernon, Texas and

Wilbarger and Wise Co. Texas Federal Census records for 1900, 1910, 1920, and 1930.
5. Cottondale Cemetery records, near Paradise, Texas.
6. Huddleston family Bible. Julia Huddleston Mosely researcher.
7. Barbara Stear, Perry Jordan descendant, research and Keith Jordan, Perry Jordan descendant.
8. Barbara Yancey Hall and Keith Jordan family records.
9. Marriage records from family Bibles and county courthouses at Wise Co., Anderson Co., Houston
   Co., and Hood Co. Texas.
10. Crockett Newspapers 1853-1896. P. 201 (August 2, 1895, vol. 6 #26)
11. Hood Co. Texas tax records and Gladow private collection of family letters.
12. Marriage records of Hood Co., Texas.
13. 1900 Federal Census for Brazoria Co., Texas.
14. Penny Jordan, William C. Jordan descendant, research.
15. Penny Jordan, William C. Jordan descendant, research.
16. 1900, 1910, 1920, 1930 Federal Census reports for Brazoria Co., Texas.
17. Huddleston family Bible. Julia Huddleston Mosely researcher.
18. Percilla Evergreen Cemetery records, Percilla, Texas.

Chapter 22
1. Ferguson Family Records. Laura Broughton researcher.
2. Ferguson Family Records. Laura Broughton researcher.

Chapter 23
1. Ferguson Family Records. Laura Broughton researcher.
2. Samuel A. Crume family Bible record.
3. Letter from S.A. Crume to Nora Ferguson 9/20/1903. Gladow private collection of family letters.
4. Samuel A. Crume family Bible record.
5. Ferguson Family Records. Laura Broughton researcher. Also Ferguson/Crume family letters from Gladow private collection.
6. Percilla Evergreen Cemetery records, Percilla, Texas.

7. Letter from Ella Ferguson to Nora Crume 4/18/1934. Gladow Collection of Family Letters .

8. Martha Ann Jordan Huddleston Bible record and Wise Co. newspaper account.

9. Martha Ann Jordan Huddleston Bible record and an article from Wise County Messenger under Local News, 14 April 1905.

10. Squires family records and Confederate Cemetery, Alvin, Texas, records.

11. Confederate Cemetery, Alvin, Texas, records.

12. 1900, 1910, 1920 Federal Census records for Greer Co., Oklahoma.

13. Account of Oliver Jordan, grandson to Perry L. Jordan. Leon Jordan Family Page. www.myfamily.com. 3 May 2007. Also, Caitrin Muldoon research in 2008.

14. Perry L. Jordan death certificate. Soniat Leonce Memorial Mercy Hospital records. New Orleans City Archives. New Orleans, Louisiana.

15. Caitrin Muldoon cemetery research. New Orleans Public Library. New Orleans, Louisiana

16. Account of Oliver Jordan, grandson to Perry L. Jordan. Leon Jordan Family Page online. www.myfamily.com 3 May 2007.

17. Perry L. Jordan death certificate. Soniat Leonce Memorial Mercy Hospital records. New Orleans City Archives. New Orleans, Louisiana.

18. Barbara Yancy Hall and Keith Jordan family records.

19. Gladow research trip to New Mexico. September 2007.

20. Blum, Catton, Morgan, Schlesinger, Stampp, and Woodward. The National Experience. New York: Harcourt and Brace, 1963. Pages 430, 431, 444.

www.ingramcontent.com/pod-product-compliance
Lightning Source LLC
Chambersburg PA
CBHW050354030726
47503CB00006B/1847